THUNDER DOG

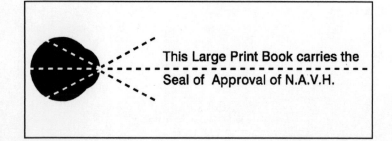
This Large Print Book carries the
Seal of Approval of N.A.V.H.

THUNDER DOG

THE TRUE STORY OF A BLIND MAN, HIS GUIDE DOG, AND THE TRIUMPH OF TRUST AT GROUND ZERO

MICHAEL HINGSON
WITH SUSY FLORY

THORNDIKE PRESS
A part of Gale, Cengage Learning

GALE
CENGAGE Learning·

Detroit • New York • San Francisco • New Haven, Conn • Waterville, Maine • London

GALE
CENGAGE Learning™

ALL RIGHTS RESERVED
Thorndike Press® Large Print Core.
The text of this Large Print edition is unabridged.
Other aspects of the book may vary from the original edition.
Set in 16 pt. Plantin.

LIBRARY OF CONGRESS CATALOGING-IN-PUBLICATION DATA

Hingson, Michael, 1950–
  Thunder dog : the true story of a blind man, his guide dog, and the triumph of trust at Ground Zero / by Michael Hingson with Susy Flory.
    p. cm.
  Includes bibliographical references.
  ISBN-13: 978-1-4104-4130-0 (hardcover)
  ISBN-10: 1-4104-4130-X (hardcover)
  1. Hingson, Michael, 1950– 2. September 11 Terrorist Attacks, 2001—Personal narratives. 3. Blind—United States—Biography. 4. Human-animal relationships. 5. Large type books. I. Flory, Susy, 1965– II. Title.
HV6432.7.H54 2011b
974.7'1044092—dc23
                                        [B] 2011027789

Published in 2011 by arrangement with Thomas Nelson, Inc.

Printed in the United States of America
1 2 3 4 5 6 7 15 14 13 12 11

For Karen, my best friend, my world, and the rock who kept me grounded after 9/11.

For Hazel tenBroek. Hazel, I never got to meet Chick, but through you and your stories, I got to know and admire him and his teachings. For a guy who university intellectuals said could never be a law student due to blindness, he certainly went on to become one of the most respected constitutional law scholars in the U.S. And to think he put his wisdom to work founding and building the National Federation of the Blind. Thank you for sharing him with me and so many others over the past quarter century.

— Michael

For Gini Monroe, my favorite cowgirl, friend, and mentor.

— Susy

CONTENTS

FOREWORD

BY LARRY KING

The sighted can only imagine what it is like to be blind. Close your eyes for a minute or two and walk through your house. For a moment, imagine it for a lifetime. Then specifically imagine being with your trusted guide dog, Roselle, working seventy-eight floors above the ground at the World Trade Center on 9/11/2001.

Thunder Dog is an incredible story of Michael Hingson and Roselle as they descend down those seventy-eight floors, helping dozens of others to escape a collapsing building. Down a stairway, desperate but calm at the same time. You will read of unforgettable moments, reflecting the blind experience with the emphasis on the senses rather than the visual. You will live again the tragedy and triumph of September 11.

Thunder Dog celebrates the power of the human and animal bond. And, we all can learn life lessons from this incredible story.

I had the honor of hosting Michael on *Larry King Live* five different times, and each time, he brought his guide dog with him. Viewers relived the story over and over again and never seemed to get enough. Since then, Michael has become an international hero with appearances all over the world. He has been honored by many organizations, and in July 2010 was the keynote speaker for the National Federation of the Blind's annual conference in Dallas.

Chapter by chapter of this intriguing work will keep you spellbound. You will relive 1,463 steps as a blind man and his dog triumph over adversity. Settle in, for you are about to read a page-turner.

INTRODUCTION
THE REAL STORY

"I'm sorry," the doctor said. "He is permanently and totally blind. There is nothing we can do for him."

George and Sarah Hingson looked at each other, devastated. Their six-month-old son, Michael, was a happy, strawberry blond baby boy, healthy and normal in every way except one. When the Hingsons switched on a light or made silly faces, Michael did not react. Ever.

Michael Hingson was born in 1950, and he was fifty-nine days early. Back then, standard medical procedure was to put a premature baby in a sealed incubator and pump in pure oxygen until the baby's lungs matured. The practice had been in place for years and resulted in an epidemic of blindness in preterm babies born before thirty-two weeks gestation. An eye disease called *retinopathy of prematurity* (ROP), formerly called *retrolental fibroplasia,* was to blame.

11

Arnall Patz, a doctor and research professor at Johns Hopkins University, discovered the cause of ROP. It turned out that extreme oxygen therapy caused blood vessels in the back of the eye to constrict. The eye, in an attempt to compensate, produced a tangled mess of blood vessels that leaked blood, scarring and subsequently destroying the retina.

Mr. and Mrs. Hingson had watched as the doctor dilated Michael's eyes, then examined each retina with a special lighted instrument called an *indirect ophthalmoscope* to determine how far the retinal blood vessels had grown. The prognosis for ROP is indicated by the stage. A diagnosis of stage 1 or 2 means the condition is less severe and will not lead to blindness. The higher the stage, the worse the prognosis. Michael was diagnosed as stage 4, meaning almost total retinal detachment, resulting in nearly complete loss of vision. The retina functions much like film in a camera, creating an image of the visual world in layers of neurons and synapses that capture light for the brain to encode and process. No retinal function means no visual information is transmitted to the brain. Michael's condition was irreversible.

Before Dr. Patz proved his controversial

theory in clinical trials, funded by money borrowed from his brother, more than ten thousand premature babies in the United States went blind between 1941 and 1953. Michael was one of those babies. So were actor Tom Sullivan, musician Stevie Wonder, and National Federation of the Blind president Dr. Marc Maurer. So many children were blinded in the early '50s that the average age of blind people in America dropped from seventy to sixty-five years.

"My best suggestion is that you send him to a home for the blind," the doctor continued after examining Michael. "The specialists there will be able to take care of him." The words took on edges and cut deep grooves of shock and grief into the Hingsons' hearts. "He will never be able to do anything for himself because of his blindness. If you keep him at home, he will only be a burden on your family."

Like most people, the Hingsons had never really been around a blind person before. But they were down-to-earth people who thought for themselves and made up their own minds. George, a self-taught television repairman with an eighth-grade education, and Sarah, a high school graduate with a beautician's license, decided to ignore the doctor. They loved Michael just the same as they loved his two-year-old brother, Ellery. No matter what the experts said, they were not going to send their beloved younger son away to a strange place far from home and family. There had to be a better way. Instinctively, the Hingsons knew that sight was not the only pathway to learning.

From the beginning, Michael was treated no differently from his brother. He was encouraged, nurtured, and loved. He was expected to grow and learn like any other child. He was allowed to explore the neighborhood on his own two feet, on his bicycle, and then with a guide dog. He never went to a school for the blind or lived in a community set apart. He never felt handicapped or disabled. He knew he was different, but he decided not to let it stop him. Ultimately, through his parents' decision to ignore the doctor's strongly worded recommendation, Michael was given the chance to grow up and find his own way in a world not set up for someone like him.

This is the story of a man blind from birth who triumphed over adversity throughout his life. His hard-won survival skills and his feisty, can-do spirit prepared him to survive the World Trade Center attacks in a seventy-eight-story stairwell descent with his guide dog, Roselle. Michael's blindness didn't stop him from shocking the neighbors by riding his bicycle through the streets of Palmdale, California, as a child, and on September 11 his blindness became an asset as he survived and helped others during the worst terrorist attack ever on American soil.

Yet, there's more. "The real story, in my mind, isn't how I got out of the World Trade Center," said Michael. "It's how I got there in the first place."

Forty-seven years after the birth of Michael Hingson, a yellow Labrador retriever puppy was born in the whelping unit of Guide Dogs for the Blind in San Rafael, California. The puppy's name was Roselle, and she, too, was blind from birth. But sometime between her third and fourth week, she opened her eyes. On September 11, 2001, she saved Michael's life. This is Roselle's story too.

1
DAY OF THUNDER

> The bond with a dog is as lasting as the
> ties of this earth can ever be.
>   KONRAD LORENZ

September 11, 2001: I can feel her body
quivering. It's twelve thirty in the morning,
and Roselle is afraid of the thunder. Again.

Drowsy, I prop myself up on one elbow
and reach down to stroke her back, then
touch her ears. I finger their velvety soft-
ness. She reaches up and noses my hand.
Usually her nose feels cool and wet, but this
time it feels warm. She's panting, and her
damp, foggy breath hangs in the air between
us.

I hear the rhythmic breathing of Karen,
my wife. *Good, she's still asleep.*

Roselle's quivering becomes shaking, and
I know I'll have to get up. I lie back for a
moment and listen. I hear the wind testing
the windows but nothing else yet. Roselle

17

knows a storm is brewing. She usually gets nervous about thirty minutes before the thunder rolls in.

I yawn and rub my face, trying to wake up. My alarm is set for 5:00, and I realize that by the time I get up with Roselle, wait out the storm with her, and get her back to bed, I'm not going to get much sleep. She stands up and begins to pant again. I sit up and rub Roselle's chin and neck, then push my feet into my slippers and stand up, grabbing my robe. Roselle rubs against my legs, happy that she won't have to face this storm alone. Her powerful Labrador retriever tail slaps against my knees once or twice as I follow her out of the room.

We head down the hallway, partly open to the first floor, then down sixteen stairs. The wooden banister feels cooler down toward the bottom. I remember hearing yesterday on the news that this storm is a cold one, blowing down from Canada and bringing the first touch of autumn to Westfield, New Jersey.

Roselle's nails tap rhythmically as she crosses the oak floor in the entryway, passes the elevator door, and heads down the steps to the basement. I follow, listening for differences in the air that keep me oriented to the three-dimensional floor plan of our house.

I first began to hear my surroundings when I was four years old. Someone gave me a kiddie car that I could drive around the apartment. I quickly learned to work the pedals and tore through the rooms at high speed. One day, while out for a spin in the living room, I drove right into the coffee table. The hood of the car was just the right height to slide underneath, and my face slammed into the edge of the table. One hospital emergency room visit and three stitches in my chin later, I faced the wrath of Mom. I suppose she could have taken away the car to make sure I never had another accident, but she didn't. "Mike, you're going to have to do a better job of watching where you're going," she said. A funny thing to say to a blind kid, but what she meant was that I should *listen* better. So I did.

Thanks in part to Mom's encouragement, in part to my just working at it, and in large part to the desire to avoid more trips to the emergency room, I began to pay more attention to what I could tell about my surroundings through my ears. And somehow I learned to hear the coffee table as I approached it. I could hear a change as I passed from one room to another. When I walked, I could hear a doorway. As I continued to race around in my pedal car, my confidence grew, and I learned to get beyond the need for eyesight. How many other four-year-olds can race their pedal cars around the house at high speed in the pitch dark? Not the light-dependent ones.

As I follow Roselle down the stairs to my basement office, I begin to hear the first deep rumbles of the approaching thunderstorm. Roselle dives under my desk and begins panting again, this time faster and louder. She is one of the most easygoing dogs I've ever known, but thunder spooks her. It's funny, though; Roselle has guided me during storms, and even though she doesn't like it, her guide dog training prevails and she guides well.

No one knows for sure why some dogs are terrified of thunderstorms. It may be that they are more sensitive to drops in barometric pressure. Or perhaps, because dogs hear at much higher and lower frequencies, they are simply hearing the storm before we do. Another possibility is that dogs can smell a storm. Lightning ionizes air with the formation of ozone, which has a characteristic metallic smell.[1] But more likely it has to do with changes in the static electric field that precedes a storm. An electrical engineer named Tom Critzer had a dog named Cody with a severe storm phobia much like Roselle's, so he designed a cape with a special metallic lining that discharges the dog's fur and shields it from the static charge buildup. I don't have a magical thunder cape for Roselle but I do crank up the volume of a radio news program to help mask the rumbling and booming.

As we wait through the storm together in the dark, Roselle cocooned at my feet, I turn on my computer and do some work to pass the time. Between the noise of the radio, my fingers tapping on the keyboard, and the rhythmic mutter of my screen reader, Roselle stops shaking, and I can sense her body starting to relax. I don't mind having the extra time to finish preparing for my morning meeting. We're expecting fifty guests for four sales training sessions, and as regional sales manager, I'm in charge of the presentation.

An hour and a half later, the thunderstorm has passed, and Roselle and I head back upstairs to bed. In less than six hours, we'll be at the World Trade Center.

We have a big day ahead.

2
1,463 STAIRS

It was one of those moments in which
history splits, and we define the world as
"before" and "after."
NEW YORK TIMES EDITORIAL,
SEPTEMBER 12, 2001

Roselle is under my desk again. This time
she's not quaking in fear but snoozing, as
only dogs can, in utter relaxation. I'm
scrambling to get ready for the morning
sales training sessions.

It's already been a very busy morning.
Between sitting up with Roselle during the
storm and then getting up just a few hours
later, at 5 a.m., I almost wish I'd had black
coffee instead of my usual PG tips tea, but I
am a tea drinker first and foremost.

Because of the scheduled meetings, I had
set my alarm for a little earlier than usual. I
needed to get to work early and make sure
everything was perfect for both the presen-

tation and the breakfast. I was looking forward to serving what I thought were the best ham and cheese croissants in New York City, ordered from the forty-fourth-floor Port Authority cafeteria called the Sky Dive.

While I'd shaved, showered, and dressed, Roselle had continued sleeping on her blanket next to the bed. *She's probably still worn out from dealing with the thunderstorm.* I let her sleep as long as I could. When it was time to go downstairs and eat, Roselle tracked my movements as usual, running ahead of me down the hallway and then downstairs to the kitchen. Since we did not have a fenced-in yard, I first took her outside on leash to relieve herself then came back in and turned on the TV. While I started in on a bowl of Special K, I listened to the news. My mind was on the morning meetings, but in the background I heard reports on the primaries; by the end of the day we'd know who was going to replace Mayor Giuliani. I got up and let Roselle back in. She grabbed her favorite Nylabone and played quietly while I finished breakfast.

A few minutes before six, I called Roselle and buckled up her harness. She has a pixie-like personality, energetic and fun loving. She plays whenever she can and works when she has to. But the leather guide dog harness is like Roselle's uniform; when she wears it, her behavior changes. She becomes less bouncy, more focused, and she always takes her job seriously. She demands that I do my job too. And she loves being part of a team.

Charlie, the owner of Happy Fox Taxi, picked us up for the ten-minute cab ride to the New Jersey Transit station. We waited at the station for the 6:18 train, but the public address system announcement said the train would be fifteen minutes late. This was a surprisingly rare occurrence, especially disappointing on a day I had planned to arrive early in New York. After two more announcements of additional delays, the train finally arrived. The train was stuffed full of passengers, all equally annoyed, and our arrival at the Newark station couldn't happen too soon.

In Newark we immediately caught a PATH train headed for the World Trade Center. PATH stands for Port Authority Trans-Hudson and provides rail service between New York City and New Jersey. The tracks cross the Hudson River through century-old cast iron tubes that rest on the river bottom under a thin layer of silt and then continue through tunnels under the streets of Manhattan. We got off the train at the World Trade Center PATH station, which connected to the World Trade Center towers via an underground concourse and shopping station. The concourse connected the Twin Towers and was like a city, always bustling with people hurrying to work or going in and out of the restaurants, bars, and shops. We took our usual route through the underground parking lot on the fourth sublevel to an elevator that took us to the lobby of the North Tower, also known as Tower 1. The electronic security unit scanned my ID card, then Roselle and I entered the elevator.

I loved working in the World Trade Center. The Twin Towers dominated the building complex, made up of seven buildings and a concourse on sixteen acres of land. The last building in the project was completed in 1973. For one year, Towers 1 and 2 were the tallest buildings in the world. Each tower rose 1,353 feet and had 110 stories and 21,800 windows. Building components included 200,000 tons of steel, 425,000 cubic yards of concrete, and 600,000 square feet of glass window area. Together the two towers weighed 1.5 million tons. New Yorkers loved to brag that the World Trade Center even had its own zip code.

Roselle and I got off the elevator at the

78th floor. I unlocked the door to 7827, the office suite for Quantum/ATL, a Fortune 500 company that provided data protection and network storage systems. I served as the regional sales manager and head of operations in New York.

Our office suite consisted of four large rooms, side by side, measuring twenty-seven feet from hallway to the window wall over-looking southwest New York City. First was a small reception area. Beyond that were some tables and the ATL P-3000, our mas-sive tape backup system; it was about 6 feet tall and weighed over 1,300 pounds. Through a door to the left was my office, also used for product demonstration, file storage, and housing our computer server. To the right was a conference room with an eleven-foot table, and further right was an office where the sales reps had desks.

Just five seconds after we arrived, so did the breakfast deliveryman. I helped him unpack and organize the hot plates, pastries, bagels, coffee, and ham and cheese crois-sants in the conference room. He left quickly, on to his next delivery.

A few minutes later, David Frank, a Quantum colleague, arrived, along with six people from Ingram Micro, a company we did business with. He had helped organize

26

the day's seminars and would be attending the meeting. David was a tall, quiet, thoughtful man from our California headquarters.

Roselle and I welcomed them all, then I went back to work setting up the conference room and testing out the presentation on my laptop. Roselle snuggled into her favorite spot under my desk. This was her usual office hangout when not performing her self-assigned duty as greeter.

A little after eight, one of the Ingram people left to return to the lobby to meet and direct others as they arrived. This left five guests in the conference room. David and I worked in my office on a spreadsheet list of attendees, making a few additions and corrections as we confirmed names. We were preparing to print out a final list on Quantum stationery to fax downstairs to the WTC security people when I realized I was out of stationery.

I carefully slid my feet out from under Roselle's sleepy head. Then, just as I stand up and turn to the supply cabinet to get some more letterhead, I hear a tremendous BOOM! It is 8:46 a.m. The building shudders violently, then starts to groan and slowly tip to the southwest. In slow motion, the tower leans over something like twenty feet.

I grew up in earthquake country near the San Andreas Fault in Southern California, so my first instinct is to go and stand in the doorway, but I know this is no earthquake. Roselle stays put under my desk while David clutches it for support. Ceiling tiles fall to the floor. We are both confused. "What could that have been?" David and I ask.

Was it an explosion? Something hitting the building? What could make it tilt that way?

Could it be an attack? No, it doesn't make sense to put a bomb that high up. It must be some kind of a gas explosion.

As we talk, the building continues tilting. Disaster seems imminent. Another few seconds and I fear the building will fall over and we will plummet to the street. *God, don't let this building tip over,* I pray silently.

Tearfully, David and I say good-bye. I'm pretty sure I'm going to die.

Then slowly, miraculously, the tilting stops and the building begins to right itself. The whole episode lasts about a minute. Just then, Roselle decides to wake up from her nap. She emerges from under my desk and quietly looks around. I can't even imagine what she is thinking, but I emerge from the doorway and grab her leash to make sure we won't be separated. I have no idea what just happened, but I'm grateful to be alive.

David looks out the window behind my desk and shouts, "Oh, my God!" The windows above us have blown out, and there is smoke and fire and millions of pieces of burning paper falling through the air. I hear debris brushing past the windows.

What we didn't know until much later is that American Airlines Flight 11, a Boeing 767 leaving Boston for Los Angeles, had been hijacked. Five men affiliated with Al-Qaeda, a Muslim terrorist organization spearheaded by Osama bin Laden, had broken into the cockpit and taken over the plane. The hijacker-pilot, a thirty-three-year-old Egyptian man named Mohammed Atta, flew the commercial jet into our building at the speed of 500 miles an hour, cutting through floors 93 to 99. Loaded with ninety-two people and around 10,000 gallons of jet fuel, the plane blasted into the North Tower with a force equal to 480,000 pounds of TNT.[1] The shock registered a magnitude of 0.9 on a seismograph at Columbia University, equal to that of a small earthquake.

The impact created a huge fireball. As the plane plowed through the building, it created a cloud of jet fuel that ignited into a firestorm, burning an estimated 1,000 to

3,000 gallons of jet fuel.[2] An instant inferno, the blaze was so intense it drove temperatures as high as 2,000 degrees.[3] The impact also caused acute structural damage, demolishing some thirty-five exterior columns between floors 94 and 98 and destroying portions of those floors.

Although the impact was more than a dozen floors above us and on the other side of the building, our office is a mess. The swaying of the tower caused the contents of the office to hit the floor along with ceiling tiles and building materials.

I hear our guests screaming in the conference room.

David yells, "We have to get out of here NOW!"

"I agree," I say. "But let's slow down and do it the right way." I want to get our guests out first then follow after we close up the office. I'd attended many of the World Trade Center emergency training sessions, and we did fire drills every six months. I run over the guidelines in my mind. *Avoid the elevators. Take the stairs. And don't panic.*

Don't panic. Some may think that might seem easy for me to say, since I can't see the flames, smoke, and debris out the window like David can. Here's the blind

guy, telling David to do something contrary to what his eyes and his instincts are telling him. I have a good imagination, and I understand what's going on as much as anyone else could understand such an unexpected and catastrophic event.

But what David doesn't understand is that I have a piece of information he does not have. When the debris began to fall and the flames leaped out of the floors above us, and even while the people in the conference room screamed, Roselle sat next to me, as calm as ever. She does not sense any danger in the flames, smoke, or anything else that is going on around us. If she had sensed danger, she would have acted differently. But she does not. I choose to trust Roselle's judgment and so I will not panic. Roselle and I are a team.

We direct our guests to evacuate using the stairwell, and I ask David to go with them to make sure they find the stairs. While he's gone, I call Karen. "There's been an explosion of some sort. We're okay, but we're leaving the building now." She's anxious, so I keep my voice calm. "David, Roselle, and I are together. We're going to take the stairs." I tell her I will call again as soon as possible, but I have to go.

David returns and we set to work shutting

down our computer servers and demo libraries. At this point we have no idea what has happened and when we'll be allowed back in and we want to protect our data. I figure if firefighters are going to come in with fire hoses, it's best if we cut the power to minimize water damage. However, we get anxious and abandon this idea because it's taking too long to move each piece of equipment to reach the individual power plugs. The minutes we save by deciding to leave now will turn out to be important later.

It's time to leave. I strap on my briefcase and clutch Roselle's harness. "Forward," I say, softly.

Forward is used when setting off with the dog in harness, and it's one of the very first commands all guide dogs are taught when training begins. You stand with your left foot out alongside the dog first, then synchronize the verbal command "Forward" with the forward hand signal, a short forward motion with the right hand. You wait for the dog to start pulling and when you feel the pull on the harness handle, you take the first step with your right foot.

We move out as one, and Roselle guides me carefully through the debris. She stays calm and focused even with things falling on top of her. David, Roselle, and I walk quickly out of the office and head out into the central corridor. People are running around. There is confusion, smoke, and noise.

Each tower has three stairwells. We head for Stairwell B, in the center. Safety is somewhere down below and 1,463 stairs are the only way out.

Forward.

3
MY OTHER SOUL MATE

A dog is the only thing on earth that loves
you more than he loves himself.

JOSH BILLINGS

The atmosphere is chaotic as people hurry
to escape the burning skyscraper. When we
come out of the office door, we take a right.
Across the hall from us are more offices. We
hustle down the hall, which forms the side
of one of the two inner squares of the 78th
floor. At the end of the hall, we turn left,
walk down another hall, and emerge into
the sky lobby.

Roselle walks with confidence, and so do
I. Although I've had guide dogs since I was
fourteen years old, I'm very aware that Roselle and I are a fairly new partnership;
we've been working together for only
twenty-one months.

It takes at least a year to forge a good
relationship with a guide dog. It's like a

marriage. Both sides have to get to know each other. I study my dog and my dog studies me, and over time we learn to read each other's thoughts and feelings. Trust begins to develop, and we become interdependent, much like a surgical team or police partners who put their lives in each other's hands. I trust Roselle with my life every day. She trusts me to direct her. And today is no different, except the stakes are higher.

I hear a few people milling around the smoky 2,600-square-foot Sky Lobby as David, Roselle, and I pass through. Even if I had ignored my emergency training from numerous drills conducted by the Port Authority and had attempted to take one of the elevators, it would have been a waste of precious minutes because all of the elevators in the North Tower had been rendered inoperative by the crash. Plus, I know that all of the central elevator shafts stretch from bottom to top. The whole center of both World Trade Center towers is hollow, two outer sheaths of steel supporting almost half the building's total weight. The buildings are lighter, flexible, and more efficient than older New York skyscrapers, such as the Empire State Building.[1] But those long, hollow elevator shafts also provide a conduit for fire and gases, so there is no way we are even going to try. As we walk quickly by the elevators, David mentions that the dark green marble trim around the elevator doors is cracked and buckling.

The 78th floor is different from most other floors in the World Trade Center because it happens to contain one of the North Tower's two "sky lobbies," where people change elevators to get to the upper stories. On a normal workday like this one, twelve large express elevators carry people from the ground floor up to the 78th floor without stopping. The elevators are huge. I used to joke about taking one over as an office. The elevators travel at twenty-two miles per hour, and the ride takes forty-eight seconds; I had timed it. Once you make it to the sky lobby, you switch, taking one of a number of smaller elevators to get to the upper floors. In all, there are ninety-seven passenger elevators and six freight elevators in each of the two towers.

While our smoke-filled sky lobby is relatively intact, it is a different story for the South Tower. In our sister building, the 78th floor elevator lobby would become a place where "life and death intersected most violently."[2] Just sixteen and a half minutes after the first plane crashed into our tower, United Airlines Flight 175 from Boston would crash directly into the 78th floor of Tower 2 next door. There are an estimated two hundred people in the sky lobby on their way out of the south building, and most of them will not make it out alive. Later, *USA Today* reporters Martha Moore and Dennis Cauchon would write, "A deafening explosion and a searing blast of heat ripped through the lobby. The air turned black with smoke. Flames burst out of elevators. Walls and the ceiling crumbled into a foot of debris on the floor. Shards of glass flew like thrown knives."[3]

This second blast flung people through the air. Survivors, burned and bleeding, woke up to a floor covered with debris, dangling steel beams, and a deluge of water from the fire sprinklers. Just like in our tower, the elevators in Tower 2 were rendered inoperable; in addition, two of the three stairwells were destroyed. Only Stairwell A was open and the few sky lobby survivors used it to escape, joining others on lower floors in descent.

Our sky lobby seems safe for now, although a fire is raging somewhere above us. The copious amounts of thick, black smoke are evidence of a fire fed by ample fuel, with flames burning at temperatures somewhere in the range of 1,300 to 1,400 degrees Fahrenheit. We still don't know what has caused the fire or even the initial impact and explosion, but the adrenaline-charged voices around us speed up my steps. The closest stairwell to us is Stairwell B. It's right in the center of the lobby, between the local elevators, the smaller ones that access the upper floors. Roselle stops at the door to the stairwell, just as she always does. She positions her body to the left of the door so I can reach out and open it. Six or seven people surround us in a loose group, and taking turns, David, Roselle, and I enter the stairwell. Roselle pauses at the top of the stairs. Through the harness I can feel her look up at me for direction. She is calm, standing quietly. I wonder what she's thinking.

"Forward," I say with confidence. But my mind immediately begins to wander. *What are we getting ourselves into? How many people are already in this stairwell trying to leave at the same time? How long is it going to take us to get out?*

My right hand clutches the rail attached to the wall while my left hand grips Roselle's leather leash and the leather-covered handle on her guide dog harness. She can relax a bit now; her job at this point is to watch the people around us and alert me to any hazards both below and above.

Dogs usually do not worry too much about what might be located above their heads. Because of their strong sense of smell, they tend to travel nose to the ground, decoding the world through scents both fresh and stale. Guide dog training is designed to prompt dogs to look up and watch for anything that might hit a blind person in the upper body, including tree branches, scaffolding, mailboxes, signs, and protrusions from vehicles and buildings.

But dogs, just like people, tend to lapse into old habits and instincts, so when my guide dog occasionally runs me into a bush or a mailbox, I pause, loop back around, and politely ask her to try it again. The dog usually guides perfectly the second time around and understands when we do a repeat that she needs to pay attention to something missed the first time.

I did have one guide dog, a golden retriever named Holland, who was a bit of a goof. He once ran me into the same mailbox several times. I was walking down a sidewalk with my parents and a mailbox jutted out over the sidewalk. Holland walked under the mailbox and my hand crashed into it.

We turned around and did it again. Then again. By the fourth time, I knew Holland was running me into it deliberately. Maybe he was having an off day. That last time, just as I was about to hit the mailbox again, I dropped the harness and jerked the leash, pulling him over toward me. He banged his head on the mailbox. I could almost feel him thinking, *This isn't working anymore.* The next time around, he nudged me over to the right so he could clear the mailbox. Problem solved.

Roselle had never done anything like that, though. As much as she likes to have fun, the harness creates a transformation. Her brow furrows a bit as her face takes on a look of intense concentration. She stands up straighter, tail erect, and her muscles tense as her movements become controlled and purposeful. Her senses go on high alert, and if she had antennae, they would be up. Roselle is ready to go wherever I command her to go. She is ready to work.

My life with dogs began long before I received my first guide dog. We always had dogs at my house growing up. Skeets was my aunt and uncle's collie in Chicago. Since they lived right next door to us in the same apartment building it seemed as though we shared him. In Palmdale we had Tramp and

Soxie, then Lady, and then Rudy, a dachs-hund. And finally, we got a feisty miniature dachshund named Pee Wee. Then I met a different kind of dog.

My dad was reading the newspaper one Sunday afternoon. "There's a new teacher out at Edwards Air Force Base. She's blind," he said. Dad worked out on the base as an electrical engineer. "Her name is Sharon Gold, and she's been hired as a school-teacher for children of military personnel on base." The article went on to mention her guide dog. My parents were intrigued. We had never been around a blind person with a guide dog before, and they decided to invite her over to dinner. So one Sunday afternoon, Sharon came over with her Ger-man shepherd, Nola. Sharon came in, greeted us, then unharnessed Nola and set her free in the backyard to play with me. "She likes to run, Michael."

Boy, did she. Nola was a typical German shepherd — large, intense, and energetic. We hit it off and in a few minutes we were running around the backyard together. At one point I grabbed onto her collar to try out the guide dog thing, and she dragged me across the grass. I think I did a few face plants. With her harness off, and because she could tell I had no idea what I was doing or how to use the guide dog commands, Nola was deep in dog play mode. Clearly, I had a lot to learn.

I loved Nola just because she was a big, friendly dog. And I loved Sharon because she was smart, eager to help, and blind like me. I was also curious about Sharon's relationship with Nola and how the relationship between the two worked. I wanted to be around her and Nola more, so my parents became good friends with Sharon, and she began to come over regularly for meals. Sharon saw my interest in Nola and soon began encouraging my parents to explore the idea of getting a guide dog for me. My parents were open to the idea because one day soon I would be heading off to Palmdale High School, a larger, more complex campus than I was used to. At the elementary school, the campus had been laid out in simple wings, and it was easy for me to navigate the covered walkways once I learned how to "hear" the support columns. But high school was a different story, more crowded and with a much larger, more complicated campus.

Looking back, I should have started by learning to travel with a cane first. But people sometimes have complicated feelings about the white cane, seeing it as a sign of weakness and disability or a barrier to fitting into the community. I'm not sure if my parents felt that way or not, but I never had a cane until I ordered one for myself years later.

Meeting Sharon was life changing. She was the first blind person I ever got to know well. Besides meeting a guide dog and handler for the first time, I learned three other important things. First, Sharon was out in the community, teaching, not stuck at home feeling sorry for herself and letting others take care of her. She had a job, and she was good at it. *If she can do it, then I can do it.* Second, I realized there was life beyond the dusty streets of Palmdale. I knew I wanted to be a part of it. And last, I realized there were many other blind people in the world besides me. Of course I had known I wasn't the only blind person, but sometimes I felt very alone. Growing up I didn't have any other blind friends. I'm not sure if that was good or bad. Looking back, there were probably pluses and minuses to growing up outside the blind community because I didn't really think of myself as blind. Perhaps mainstreaming forced me to find new and innovative ways of doing things in order to succeed. But at the same time, I didn't have the support and friendship of others like me who were wiser and more experienced than I was.

I found out I was getting a guide dog one day while I was outside jumping rope in my eighth grade physical education class. Usually I didn't get to participate much in PE, but I happened to be excellent at jumping rope.

A man walked up to me. "Hello, Michael. I am Larry Reese from Guide Dogs for the Blind." I was so shocked, I let the rope drop. Mr. Reese had driven down to Palmdale from the Guide Dogs campus in San Rafael, which was just north of San Francisco on the Marin Peninsula. It was about an eight-hour drive in those days.

"Michael, we're looking forward to having you come and get a guide dog," he said. *What?* I didn't even know my parents had applied. Maybe they didn't want me to be disappointed if I had been turned down. I was just fourteen, and the rule was that you had to be sixteen to get a guide dog. For some reason, Guide Dogs bent the rules for me.

In late June, my parents sent Ellery off to Boy Scout camp and then my dad, mom, and I drove up to San Rafael, where they dropped me off at Guide Dogs for the Blind. Back then it was surrounded by roll-

44

ing green hills and undeveloped land out in the middle of nowhere. As we drove down the gravel road leading into the campus, I was practically wiggling with excitement. I had hardly ever been out of Southern California, and it all seemed like a big adventure. I wasn't too worried about getting homesick; after all, I had survived a couple of previous stints at summer camp. And I was far too excited about getting a guide dog to be nervous.

My parents dropped me off on Sunday, and I spent the day exploring the eleven-acre campus. At the front of the campus was an administration building. Off to one side was a small dorm with eight double rooms. On the other side was a house for the executive director. There was also a dining room, a common room with a small television and an out-of-tune zither, and a swimming pool. At the back were the dog kennels.

Class started the very next day and I was the youngest person by far. The average age for a guide dog user is fifty-one. Being around so many adults made me slightly nervous, and I had to learn how to behave. One morning we hit town for a training session and ended up at the Downtown Lounge in San Rafael for lunch. I got up and went to the restroom and left the door open, like we did at home. I can't believe I did that, but I guess because I couldn't see anything, I didn't think about other people looking in and seeing me. Or maybe I was just an idiotic adolescent. In any case, I was quickly made aware that my bathroom etiquette needed an upgrade.

One thing I loved about the Guide Dogs campus was that every room had a record player in it for talking books, recorded on twelve-inch vinyl records. Whenever I wasn't in class or practicing, I spent my time reading books that way.

In class I learned that Guide Dogs for the Blind started with the idea of using shelter dogs as guides for blind service personnel after World War II. Blondie, a German shepherd rescued from the Pasadena Humane Society, became the guide dog for Sgt. Leonard Foulk, the first serviceman to graduate from the school in 1941.

The first skill I learned in training involved basic footwork. Guide Dogs teaches through "Juno" training, with the trainer holding the harness to simulate working with an imaginary dog named Juno. Footwork involved learning to coordinate keeping my left foot by the dog's right front paw. This may sound simple, but it isn't if you can't see the dog's foot or your own foot. I also learned the verbal commands and hand signals, how to properly use the harness and leash, and how to both correct and praise a guide dog. As a class, we also participated in lectures where we learned techniques for basic dog training and obedience, along with how to keep our dogs healthy and happy.

Three days later, I got my dog. There was an excited buzz in the air on Wednesday, also known as Dog Day. The trainers had been carefully evaluating each of us for personality (quiet or energetic? patient or hotheaded?), gait (fast or slow? small or large stride?), and physical capacity (strong or weak? young or aged?). Trainers had also studied our home environments (busy, big city or small, rural town?) and our lifestyles (frequent traveler or homebody?). Last, they had taken a close look at our day-to-day surroundings (high-rise building, crowded classrooms and hallways, or peaceful home office?). After careful consideration of every facet of both the human's and the dog's lives, Guide Dogs matched each of us up with the dog that seemed the best fit. The wise trainers knew I needed a calm, collected dog with the patience to put up with a teenager.

On Dog Day, we sat through a morning lecture about the dogs, ate a quick lunch in the dining room, then went to our rooms to wait. I was so nervous I couldn't sit still enough to listen to a talking book in order to pass the time. I sat and fidgeted, getting up to pace back and forth when I could no longer stand it. My roommate felt the same way. Finally, I was called into instructor Bruce Benzler's office.

"Mike, sit quietly," he said. "Your dog is Squire. Squire is a dark red golden retriever, about sixty-four pounds. I want you to be patient. Don't say anything. I'm going to let the dog in, and we'll see how he reacts to you."

Mr. Benzler got up and walked to the door. He opened it, and Squire walked in the room. He came straight over and started sniffing me all over. I was excited and my hands itched to pet him, but I obeyed and sat still. Squire inspected me for about thirty seconds then sat down next to me and waited. "It looks like you found a friend," said Mr. Benzler. I gave Squire a hug. My heart was pounding.

"You can take Squire back to your room now," said Mr. Benzler. "Use his leash, and ask him to heel. Then take some time to get to know each other."

Squire and I headed back to my room. I felt like I was walking on air with Squire by my side. When the door closed behind us, I sat down and talked to Squire for the next couple of hours. I'd known plenty of dogs, but I'd never met a dog before that was so mature and well trained. I felt an immediate bond with Squire. He liked me and seemed interested in me. We just seemed to fit.

Squire and I developed a partnership, and I learned how to read Squire's body language through the handle of the harness; I could almost tell what he was going to do before he did it. I think he learned to read me too. He was much more than just a pet. Squire was my best friend, and we became a team as he guided me safely through the halls of Palmdale High School for the next four years. He was a quick study. When faced with a gaggle of girls in a crowded campus hallway, Squire learned to stick his cold, wet nose under a miniskirt or two. When the girls would shriek and jump out of the way, my brother, Ellery, swore that Squire actually grinned. I suspect I almost received a few slaps and I am sure I was the subject of many angry looks, thanks to Squire.

Squire and our dachshund, Pee Wee, got along famously and wore tracks in the carpet chasing each other up and down the hallways of our house. The two dogs developed a game where Pee Wee raced down the hallway, with Squire in hot pursuit. When they got to the living room, Pee Wee bunched up his long, narrow body like a spring and jumped up on the couch. Squire would run up and grab him off the couch, flip his little sausage body over on the ground, and gnaw on his stomach, play-growling all the while.

I know Pee Wee must have missed Squire when he went with me to college. After a few years with me at UC Irvine, Squire grew old and tired. He was eleven years old and couldn't keep up with me anymore. The very worst thing about guide dogs is they don't last very long. The average guide dog only makes it as a working dog until the age of nine or ten because guiding is both physically and emotionally stressful for the dog. I loved Squire, and I think the relationship with your first guide dog is something like the first time you fall in love. Squire occupied a special corner in my heart. Forever. But it was time for him to retire, and he went to live with my parents back in Palmdale with his little buddy PeeWee. Squire lived to be fourteen years old, a good, respectable age for a golden.

After Squire retired, I headed back to San Rafael for a second time, and Guide Dogs paired me with another golden retriever named Holland. He was a good, steady guide dog. He took me through my graduate years and my first several years of employment. I tried to take advantage of his chick-magnet qualities, but most of the time women were interested only in the dog, not me.

After Holland, I got another golden, named Klondike; he guided me through much of my working life. Klondike had a bit of an overactive digestive system and sometimes filled the office conference room with a — how shall I put this? — pungent aroma. It didn't bother me; I figured it helped keep my sales force awake and alert.

Linnie was next, a light-blonde Labrador retriever. She was a wonderful dog. Whenever anyone touched her, she would stop, drop, and roll over to get her stomach scratched. We ran across actor Peter Falk once in an airport frequent-flier lounge, and he spent ten minutes on his knees on the carpet, scratching her stomach. "Linnie, I can't sit here all night," he groused in his gravelly voice, smiling big. Linnie had a sixth sense about people. In a crowd, she always went right to the person who needed some attention. She would have made a great therapy dog. Her guiding career ended abruptly when she contracted Lyme disease from a backyard tick bite. She retired in 1999 after only three years of guiding, and Karen and I kept her as a pet. Linnie became a beloved part of our family.

After Linnie, I went without a guide dog for six months, using a cane to get around New Jersey and New York City, including the World Trade Center. New York sidewalks are jam-packed, and I spent way too much money replacing broken white canes at forty dollars a pop because people didn't watch where they were going.

Then, in November 1999, Roselle entered our lives. I found myself back in San Rafael at Guide Dogs for the Blind in that same office, waiting to be matched with a new guide dog. Although this was my fifth time, I was just as nervous and excited as that first time, thirty-five years earlier. The only way I can describe the feeling of waiting for your guide dog is that it is almost exactly like standing at the front of the church in your tuxedo, waiting for the organ to play the "Wedding March" and your bride-to-be to start down the aisle. Your life will never be the same, and you will no longer be alone.

When the training supervisor let Roselle into the office to meet me, she was a bit of a busybody. She sniffed me all over then left and snuffled her way around the room. "Well, call her and see if she'll come to you," suggested the supervisor. Roselle slowly made her way back. Then she stopped and sat down next to me and didn't move again. I took her back to the room and chatted with her for a while. I petted her and played with her and we got to know each other. I quickly noticed she had two sides to her personality. She could be very calm and quiet when she was working. But when the harness came off, she became a little mischievous. She liked to steal my socks, carry them off in her mouth, and hide them, but she never chewed them up. I also noticed she snored. Like a grizzly bear.

Roselle's puppy raisers were Ted and Kay Stern, a retired couple in Santa Barbara, California, who first got her as a fuzzy, yellow, four-month-old puppy with an impish twinkle in her eye. The Sterns gave Roselle her first ten months of basic in-home obedience training and acquainted her with as many different environments as possible, including a visit to New York City at Christmastime. The hectic pace of urban life didn't seem to faze Roselle as the Sterns

53

visited packed restaurants, clattering subways, and crowded sidewalks.

At home, Kay remembered Roselle as spunky and playful. "She used to steal my slippers from the closet and run all around the house to try to play keep-away," Kay said. "She loved to play hide-and-seek with us, and I loved her crooked doggy smile. She sometimes tested limits and tried to pretend she didn't remember her lessons. She was a smart pup." They also reported her snoring, especially in church.

When we got back to New York, Roselle and Linnie became fast friends. Whenever I worked down in the basement of our house in New Jersey and I needed to take a break, I'd grab a braided Booda rope bone and play tug-of-war with the dogs. They pulled me all around the basement in my rolling office chair, banging me into walls and posts. It was something like a human pinball game and I was the ball.

Within two days of her arrival at the house, Roselle went off to work with me at the World Trade Center. Initially, we spent a lot of time exploring the building's hallways, its lobbies, and the underground shopping center. I worked hard to make sure she would not expect to always go the same way to get to a particular location within the building. I always felt it important that Roselle not be able to anticipate my commands — something that can easily happen within a confined space such as the WTC. Roselle and I made a good match; we were always up for an adventure.

But my 9/11 adventure would have very high stakes.

As Roselle and I walk together down the first few concrete stairs of Stairwell B, I begin to smell a peculiar odor. It reminds me of the smell of kerosene lanterns at Boy Scout camp. At first it's slightly pungent, though. Just a tickle. *I wonder what that smell is?* Roselle must smell it too, but she gives no sign.

More stairs, with our small group heading down. The temperature in the stairway is comfortable, not too hot or too cold. The electricity is working and the air is breathable. *But that smell . . .*

Then it hits me. As a salesman, I've flown all over the world and been through countless airports. *I know that smell. I've smelled it on the runway. I could swear it's jet fuel.*

I don't say anything yet, but my mind begins to reel. *Could a plane have hit our building?*

4
HEARING THE COFFEE TABLE

I wonder if anyone else has an ear so tuned and sharpened as I have, to detect the music, not of the spheres, but of earth, subtleties of major and minor chord that the wind strikes upon the tree branches. Have you ever heard the earth breathe?

KATE CHOPIN

The stairwell doesn't feel crowded at first. People are quiet. Focused. No one is panicking. We just want out.

Stairs are usually a breeze. If I can ride a bike or drive a car, I can certainly climb down a bunch of stairs.

When I can, I walk down with my hand on the metal railing to my right. The railing juts out from the concrete wall, which feels cool to the touch. On the left is another metal handrail, this one supported by metal balusters. On my left, Roselle matches my pace, my hand on her harness handle. David is just ahead. Our stairwell is fifty-six inches wide, a full foot wider than the two corner stairwells. This additional space allows two people to climb down the stairs side by side. Sometimes we move out and pass people on the left; sometimes people pass us. I switch Roselle from side to side as needed. Everyone is polite but focused.

Each floor has nineteen stairs split up into two flights. The first flight has ten stairs. At the bottom is a landing with a 180-degree turn, then nine more stairs. Usually I don't count stairs. It's the dog's job to pause and let me know when I get to the top of a set of stairs and when I get to the bottom. But this time I count for something to do.

Not only am I counting stairs, I'm listening carefully. My adrenaline is pumping, and I feel very alert with all of my senses heightened. As I walk, I strain to hear and decode the smallest sounds from the building. It's telling me a story, and I don't want to miss what it has to say.

Part of the story is what I am not hearing. I haven't heard any more explosions. No fire alarms have sounded. No emergency announcements have crackled through the PA system. No emergency personnel have appeared to let us know what is happening.

And no one can make phone calls. Cell phones are so ubiquitous that as a culture we are used to one-sided conversations surrounding us in almost any public place. But cell phones don't work well in our steel-and-concrete cave. So as we descend, it's mostly quiet.

The lack of cell phone reception also means we aren't getting any news from outside. It's like we're together in a bubble, isolated from whatever is going on above, below, and outside. Right now my world consists of stairs. Ten stairs, turn, nine stairs. Again. And again.

Everything feels unreal. I can't believe that just a few minutes ago I was preparing for seminars in the conference room. Now we are on the run. But whenever I become uneasy, I listen to Roselle. The tough pads of her feet cushion her steps and since we keep her nails trimmed short, her footsteps are silent. But I can hear her breathing. Although we've been walking down the stairs for just a few minutes, Roselle is beginning to pant. The temperature in the stairwell is comfortable, so she's panting not from the heat but from the exertion of her intense focus on her work.

Dogs have fewer sweat glands than people, who cool off as sweat evaporates from the surface of the skin. But canine sweat glands, located on the pads of the dog's feet and on the ears, play a smaller role in cooling. Instead, dogs pant to cool off the blood circulating through the major blood vessels of the head, which surround the nose. The surface area of the tongue also provides cooling through the evaporation of moisture in the dog's mouth. Roselle is not nervous, just warm. She's at the top of her game, walking with confidence and a spring in her step.

The fuel smell is strong on certain landings. When I first noticed it, the smell was just a hint, a whisper of danger. But now it feels heavier and fuller, a toxic stench beginning to sink into my throat and my lungs. I swallow and it feels like I'm drinking a shot of kerosene. My eyes are starting to burn too. Roselle pants a little harder. *I know she can taste it too.*

There's a reason we are inhaling the fumes of jet fuel in Stairwell B. We will learn later that when the Boeing 767 hit our building, it was carrying around ten thousand gallons of fuel, most of it in the wing tanks. The plane crashed into the north side of the building and obliterated several floors while spewing out jet fuel. The droplets atomized, forming a combustible mixture that exploded, ignited "by the enormous heat of friction, by sparks from pieces of steel, by hot engine parts, and most of all by short circuits in the wiring of the North Tower . . . The force of the explosion was so great that parts of the aircraft hurled out of the other side of the tower. After impact, bewildered passersby on a street near the World Trade Center stood around a huge cylinder of bent metal. It took a while before they realized they were looking at an aircraft engine."[1]

Although the impact generated a tremendous explosion, not all of the jet fuel was consumed, and it shot out of the fuel tanks and sprayed over the floors below, a film of fuel covering stairwells, offices, and elevator shafts "at a rate of more than a hundred miles an hour. Curtains, upholstery, and carpets soaked up the fuel like wicks."[2]

Fumes are floating along the air currents inside the building and infiltrating the ventilation system, so everyone in the stairwell can smell it now. I am the first to say it out loud. "I think the smell is jet fuel. Maybe an airplane hit our building?"

The people around us talk it over, trying to figure out what happened. We speculate that maybe there was some sort of midair collision, causing the plane to plow into our building. But we are not sure.

■ ■ ■ ■

Actually, this isn't the first time a plane hit a skyscraper in New York. In 1945, a B-25 bomber rammed into the Empire State Building, back then the world's tallest building. The pilot, a decorated veteran of more than one hundred combat missions, got lost in thick fog and slammed into the 79th floor at two hundred miles per hour. In a stroke of luck, the accident occurred on a Saturday morning without too many people in the building. Still, fourteen people died, along with the pilot and two passengers. The damage was extensive, with the bomber blasting an eighteen-by-twenty-foot hole in the building, spewing plane parts, and shattering windows. In addition, when the bomber hit, its fuel tanks exploded and started a fire on the 79th floor.

Just like us in the World Trade Center, those Empire State Building survivors took to the stairs, and some of them descended seventy flights to get out. But rescuers also used the still-working elevators for evacuation. One miraculous survivor story emerged after an Empire State Building elevator operator named Betty Lou Oliver was thrown out of her post by the impact of the plane crash and badly burned. Betty was given first aid then was put into a different elevator and sent down to meet a waiting ambulance. Disaster struck when the elevator cables, weakened by the crash, snapped, and the car plummeted a thousand feet to the basement. Strangely enough, Betty survived and was recovered when rescuers cut a hole in the car to get her out.[3]

The Empire State Building survived the crash and the fire, and the beautiful old skyscraper still stands. But I am certain the hole in our building must be much larger than just eighteen by twenty feet.

An airplane crashed into the building. Why? How could this happen? The thunderstorm is long past, and September 11 is a clear autumn day, no fog. With instrumentation and air-traffic control, no airplane should have come anywhere near the World Trade Center. *What is going on?*

As we walk down the stairs, the sound of the initial explosion reverberates in my head. The crowd on the stairs is large enough that many of the usual echoes I would hear while going between floors are muffled or gone altogether. The walls of the stairwell are the boundaries of our little world. Although our senses are on high alert, inside our cocoon it feels natural, almost hypnotic, just to continue to walk down ten stairs, turn, and then walk down the next set.

While this situation was unfamiliar, navigating down the stairwell wasn't too much of a challenge. But learning how to ride a bicycle blind was. When I was about six years old, a girl named Cindy Loveck moved into the neighborhood during the summer. The Lovecks lived across the street, a few doors down, and Cindy and I became friends. Cindy had a full-sized bike and rode it up and down the streets of our high desert town of Palmdale.

One day she offered to let me try out her bike. I didn't hesitate. After several attempts that included a number of falls and scrapes, I learned how to balance the bike on two wheels.

But once I learned to ride the bike, I had to figure out how to avoid obstacles, so I set out to use the tricks I'd learned while driving my little pedal car. Just as I learned how to hear the coffee table, I learned how to hear parked cars so I could avoid them while riding down the street. "You would click your mouth just like a bat, kick it out there, and listen for the returns," my older brother, Ellery, says now. Also, the rubbery echo of the bicycle tires rolling down the street provided me with invaluable information including sound changes as I approached parked cars and other objects. No one taught me echolocation; I just figured it out on my own.

My parents always encouraged me to go outside and play with the other kids on the street, and they never stopped me from trying new things. Soon after I learned how to ride Cindy's bike, my parents bought me a bike of my own, and I rode it for hours a day. I loved the feeling of freedom and control.

One day I came in the house from riding my bike, and my dad was on the phone.

"Well, he was just out riding his bike," he said. There was an edge to his voice. Then, a pause.

"Did he crash into anything?" Pause.

"Then what's the problem?" My dad hung up. I don't want to say he slammed down the phone, but he hung it up with some force.

It turned out that a neighbor had called to inform my dad that his son (*not the older kid who can see but the younger kid who is blind,* she had said) had been spotted riding a bicycle down the street. I guess the well-meaning neighbor thought my parents should know. But just as my parents had ignored the doctor's recommendation to send me away to a school for the blind, they ignored comments like these. No one in my family treated me like I had a disability. They expected me to do for myself. So I did.

As I mastered the art of bike riding via echolocation, I ventured farther afield in Palmdale, a town of about two thousand. I can still conjure up a map of our part of town. At the center of the grid in my mind is our house at 38710 Stanridge Avenue. Our house was between Third Street and Glenraven Street. Between the streets ran the avenues, each named with a letter of the alphabet, along with a number. The avenues were one mile apart. Our house was between Avenue Q and Avenue Q3, although it was closer to Q. So we were between Q and Q3 on the north and south, and between Third and Glenraven on the east and west.

Although I mastered riding the streets, I came home more than once to find one of my parents on the phone, hearing yet again about their blind child out riding unaccompanied around the neighborhood. The calls always ended with the neighbors hanging up in frustration. My parents never gave in, and eventually neighbors got used to the blind kid riding his bike and the lack of outrage expressed by my parents and finally stopped calling.

I spring from stubborn and self-reliant stock. I also can only hope that my parents' persistence served to educate my neighbors a little about what blind people can do. My father's can-do attitude was a huge influence on me. His name was George Hingson, and he was born in 1914 in Dewey, Oklahoma. A quiet man with a grade school education, he left home when he was just twelve or thirteen years old. I'm not sure why. To support himself, he went to work herding sheep on the Idaho-Montana border in the Bitterroot Mountains, a subrange of the Rocky Mountains. It's a beautiful, pristine wilderness with rugged peaks and steep canyons carved by glaciers, but not an easy place for a young boy to live outdoors for months at a time without home or family. Big game flourishes in the area, which means predators are about, so my father's job was to protect his flock of sheep from wolves, bobcats, and mountain lions. He used to tell us a story about accidentally cutting off his thumb with an ax then burying it in the snow for three days until he was able to get somewhere where doctors

66

could surgically reattach it. I never saw much of a scar, but he couldn't bend his thumb at the first joint. So even my dad, the tough guy who always defended me, had accidents too.

Later, Dad worked as a cowboy, ending up in Washington State. He finally realized he didn't want to chase cattle the rest of his life, so in his midtwenties he enlisted in the army. He served in the Third Infantry Division, which deployed to North Africa, Italy, Sicily, and Southern France during World War II. He was part of the Signal Corps, a branch of the service responsible for all military information and communications systems. Some of the Signal Regiment's accomplishments during World War II included developing radar and FM radio for military use. The Signal Corps also developed the first FM backpack radio, allowing front-line troops to communicate reliably and static free, thanks to frequency modulation circuits. His military training in electronics would come in very handy back in the United States.

While serving overseas, my dad became friends with a man named Sam Keith. Sam's wife, Ruthie, wrote letters to her husband and often included pictures of friends and family. One day, George happened to see a photograph of Ruthie's sister, Sarah. She was a slight woman, blonde and pretty. He was smitten and asked Sam if it would be okay for him to write to Sarah. Sam agreed, and a wartime romance flourished in a flurry of red-and-blue–striped Air Mail envelopes.

Sarah Stone was not your average girl. A street-smart and independent woman, she originally hailed from New York City. She was a high school graduate, she loved to read, and she earned a beautician's license and supported herself at a time when not many women did. She had lived and worked in both New York and California, finally ending up in Chicago. Sarah and George hit it off, and when the war was over, George went straight to Chicago and married Sarah in November 1945. These two strong and independent people fell in love and were happily married for nearly four decades, thanks to Uncle Sam, both the country and the man.

My parents set up house in an apartment on the south side of Chicago. My aunt Ruth and uncle Sam, my dad's wartime buddy, lived in a nearby apartment. Next door to Ruth and Sam lived my mom's brother, Abe, and his wife, Shirley. We were a tight family. We still are.

Dad and Uncle Abe pioneered a television repair business together back when TVs were rare and expensive. Because people invested $200 to $300 in their television sets back then ($1,500 to $3,000 in today's dollars), they were willing to spend money to keep them working. It wasn't a bad way to make a living.

My brother, Ellery, was born in 1948. Two years later, I was born on February 24, 1950, at Mount Sinai Hospital in Cook County, Chicago. I was two months early and weighed just two pounds, thirteen ounces. My mother always said I was rushing it, in a big hurry to get into the world.

The day I was born, Chicago was buried under a tremendous snowstorm, so my mom gifted me with a special, commemorative name: Michael Blizzard Hingson.

A *blizzard* usually means heavy snow and high winds, but the word can also refer to whiteout conditions. Snow and ice reflect incoming light, and objects, landmarks, and shadows are no longer discernible. Land and sky blend, and the horizon disappears into a white nothingness. True whiteouts can render a person temporarily blind. Unfortunately, my blindness would not be temporary.

When I was born, my uncle Abe and aunt

Shirley braved the storm and visited the hospital when I was just two days old. "The storm was bad," my aunt told me. "You couldn't see anything in front of you."

Babies were kept behind glass in those days. "The nurse picked you up and held you so we could see," Aunt Shirley said. "You were very, very small. You looked like a little chicken with a large head. They kept you in the incubator so your lungs could develop, and you were in the hospital for two to three months.

"When you came home," she continued, "the family thought maybe you had a cataract because one eye looked a little glassy. I went with Sarah to every possible doctor you could imagine to see what could be done."

Meanwhile, I gained weight and seemed normal in every other way.

One day, however, Aunt Shirley noticed something unusual. She was babysitting me while my parents and my brother, Ellery, were on a trip to California. "The second morning I was there," she said, "I changed your diaper and got you all fixed up. I made you some Pablum for breakfast, took you in my arms, and we sat down at the table. There were three large windows nearby with venetian blinds. The sun was coming in so bright I picked you up again and stood up to close the blinds. The sun shone on your face, right into your eyes, and you didn't blink. The light didn't bother you at all."

Aunt Shirley finished feeding me then put me in the crib. But she was horrified by what had happened. *Could Michael be blind?* She ran next door to tell my aunt Ruthie, and when my parents returned, she told them too. When I was six months old, the doctor finally made his diagnosis. I was blind, and it was irreversible. My parents announced the news to the family, and everyone cried. Briefly. Then they moved on.

From the beginning I was treated no differently than my brother. I also had my cousins around to keep me humble. Aunt Ruth and Uncle Sam had two boys, Steve and Robin. Uncle Abe and Aunt Shirley had two girls, Holly and Dava. The cousins all played together in the yard behind the apartment house, and I was allowed out with them, even when I was quite young. My parents trusted us, and we were allowed to explore the neighborhood without a grown-up in attendance. With Ellery and the cousins, I regularly headed to the candy store, where I always picked out penny pretzel sticks and orange soda pop. Sometimes I held on to someone's hand in that absentminded way kids do. Other times I followed behind. Once in a while, I led. I couldn't always find my way safely without help, but my cousins didn't make a big deal about it, and neither did I.

"I always knew you were blind," said my cousin Dava Wayman, "but I never thought of you being any different. You were doing everything my other cousins did. You were treated like any other kid. Nothing held you back."

My big brother, Ellery, used to chase me around the apartment, not taking much pity on my youth or size. He remembers strategically placing my beloved pedal car in my path then chasing me until I ran into it.

Once in a while I got to ride along on TV repair service calls with my dad, and I loved visiting the shop. One day I put my hand inside a live TV and got the shock of my life. My dad used the experience to give me my first lesson in basic electricity: never use both hands to touch a live circuit. Always keep one hand in your pocket so as not to become a ground for the current. After that, I was safe around open, running televisions.

When my parents enrolled me in kindergarten at Perry School in 1954, they decided they wanted me to learn Braille so I could learn to read and write. Back then public schools didn't offer specialized classes, but my parents, along with a group of other parents of prematurely born blind children, pushed hard for it, and the school ended up hiring a Braille teacher. I began to learn Braille, starting with the alphabet. I practiced writing on a Braille writer, a special device something like a manual typewriter that produces Braille characters on paper. I picked it up quickly, and by the end of the school year, I could read and write Braille at a good, basic level.

After kindergarten, we packed up and moved to Palmdale, California, about sixty miles north of Los Angeles, out in the Antelope Valley. My parents had yearned to live in the Golden State, and my dad found an engineering job at Plant 42, a government facility later operated by Lockheed Martin.

But at my new school in California, I was the only blind kid, and for several years I had no Braille teacher. I was at the mercy of my teachers and my parents, who had to read my assignments to me. When the other kids colored, drew pictures, or did other visual projects, I waited. And waited.

My parents knew I was bright and worked with me at home. My father was mostly self-educated, picking up electronics and electrical engineering on his own along with a few technical courses he picked up along the way. I probably learned much more from my parents than I learned at school those first few years.

My dad taught me how to do algebra in my head when I was six. I not only got the answers to the problems, but I knew why I got the answers. Mom worked with me on my other assignments and with most of my learning taking place at home, I was often bored at school. The teachers couldn't involve me because I couldn't read printed materials or look at diagrams or pictures. There were no books for me to read, and I was often left to my own devices. I felt detached and separated from the rest of the kids and often wandered over to the window and stood, listening for what was happening outside.

One day in class, the teacher asked us to draw a picture. I sat with my blank sheet of paper while the other kids drew. The teacher told me the other kids would help. I kept asking the kids at my table for help, but they were too busy with their own drawings. Finally, one boy got fed up with me, grabbed my piece of paper, and crumpled it up. He dropped it in front of me and said, "Don't bother us." I got the message. It was the first time I remember my blindness provoking hostility.

Outside of school, Palmdale was an exciting place for a boy to grow up. Edwards Air Force Base nearby was the testing ground for top-secret military aircraft with Chuck Yeager and the rest of *The Right Stuff* guys breaking through the sound barrier and creating tremendous sonic booms, often over the general's house.

At first I wandered around the quiet neighborhoods with my mom and brother, but before long I navigated the streets all by myself. I made it a game to find my way back to our house. I learned that each driveway had small but detectable differences in elevation, length, and in the number and shape of cracks. Our driveway was a bit longer and flatter than the others, and I learned to feel and hear the difference in the incline. In a perfect world, I would have learned how to use a cane at this point. But I didn't know any other blind people, and I didn't know anything about canes. Instead, my senses naturally sharpened as I explored the area, and I used touch and hearing to travel on my own.

Contrary to popular misconceptions, blind people do not magically obtain other heightened senses. We have to develop better hearing through practice, just like anyone else. And with practice, it wasn't long before I learned to walk on my own to Yucca Elementary School, three blocks from our house. Soon after that, I began riding my bike and alarming the neighbors.

Several times during my early school years, my parents were called in to meet with the principal, who would strongly recommend that I be sent to the residential school for the blind in Berkeley, California, several hundred miles north of our town. My parents always refused. They wanted me at home and in regular classrooms, "mainstreaming" me before the term had ever been coined.

Finally, the summer between third and fourth grade, the school district hired a resource teacher to provide me and a few other blind children in the area with training in Braille. Her name was Cora Hershberger, and she helped me relearn Braille. I picked it up quickly and at last I could read for myself — the door to books and to learning now open. My curiosity and imagination ignited, and I fell in love with books as I explored the world through dots on a page, just as I had explored my neighborhood by learning the cracks and bumps of the sidewalks. Those exploration techniques I learned as a child came in so handy when we had to make our way out of Tower 1. I have always felt that every life experience helps us prepare for what is to follow.

Like using my ears to hear my driveway or to avoid parked cars when riding my bike, I developed the skills I needed to navigate the World Trade Center. I am as familiar with my building as I was with the cracks in my childhood sidewalk. And my early feeling of being an outsider still makes me strive hard to be part of the community, no matter the cost. I don't rely unnecessarily on other people, and I never play the blind card.

Ten stairs, turn, nine stairs. Ten stairs, turn, nine stairs.

On the 70th floor, the stairwell ends, and we file through a door back into the building. It's quiet, the abandoned floor a ghost town. We go back into the stairwell through a different door and start back down.

I remember something a PE teacher taught me when I wanted to run faster and farther. *Count to two when you breathe in, and three when you breathe out.* I try it, synchronizing my breathing with the stair count. One, two, in; one, two, three, out.

Then the shouting starts, from somewhere above.

5
Kicked off the Bus

The whole idea of compassion is based
on a keen awareness of the
interdependence of all these living beings,
which are all part of one another, and all
involved in one another.

THOMAS MERTON

Ten floors down, sixty-eight to go, and the stairwell is beginning to fill up. People are leaving the North Tower in droves, and we form a slow but steady single-file line that snakes down. Sometimes when a door opens on a landing, we smell smoke. Most people are calm and quiet, lost in thought and focused on getting out. Every once in a while someone gets out of line, anxious, walking quickly to pass by on the left. But there is no pushing or shoving, no angry or panicky voices.

Instinctively we all keep to the right, with the left side of the stairwell open for people who, for whatever reason, need to get down in a hurry. But we have dozens of flights and hundreds of stairs yet to go, so we pace ourselves. As we walk, I let go of the banister and flip up the crystal on my watch, a Seiko quartz with raised markers at 3, 6, 9, and 12. I gently touch the hour and minute hands, and I'm shocked. It's only 8:55. That means it's been just nine minutes since the plane — if that is what it was — hit our building. *I wonder how much damage the fire has done. Is it spreading? Will it enter the stairwell?*

To help me focus, I use my watch to time our descent. Each step takes about a second, with a full flight of stairs equaling about twenty seconds of travel time. With sixty-eight floors remaining, and assuming we can keep up our current pace, it will take us just over twenty-two minutes to evacuate. However, chances are there will be some slow-downs along the way. So far we've been lucky.

The stairwell is heating up from the mass of bodies, and I begin to sweat, my dress shirt sticking to my back. Roselle is getting warmer, too, her breath heavier and faster. The air feels heavy and the jet fuel smell is still there, sometimes faint, sometimes stronger than ever. I can wonder again what it must smell like to Roselle.

Then we hear shouting from somewhere up above. "Look out!" a voice cries. "Burn victim coming through. Please let us by." I move to the right, gripping the railing, and pull on the harness, nudging Roselle in close to my legs. We stop for a moment as a knot of people rushes by. Their breathing and hurried steps tell me all I need to know. I can feel Roselle watching, her head tracking the group as they pass by and go down.

After the group passes and we start back down the stairs, I call out to David. "What did you see?"

"A woman," David says. "She is burned so bad that she doesn't even look like a human being." The group of hurried people had surrounded the woman to help her get down. Somehow she is still able to walk. She is the first injured person we've encountered, although I know there must be many more.

But where are they?

We continue down. Ten stairs, turn, nine stairs. Five minutes later there are more shouts, directing us to move aside. I pull Roselle in again as another burn victim hurries down the stairs. Again it's a woman, and David says this one looks even more horrible than the first. Deep in shock, she walks like a zombie, eyes straight ahead and expressionless. Her clothes are partly burned off, her skin blistered and separating, her blonde hair "caked in gray slime."[1]

A number of people on or near the sky lobby on our floor were sprayed with burning fuel after the plane entered our building. One of these I heard about later was a forty-four-year-old woman named Virginia DiChiara. She was in an express elevator, waiting to leave the 78th floor when the plane hit the building. Fire flashed into the elevator then left just as quickly. The lights went out and burning jet fuel dripped down through the elevator shaft and onto Virginia's shoulders and back. Roy Bell, another elevator passenger, said, "It looked like sheets of white fire, thin sheets of fire. The flame was coming through the elevator car doors from the inside out, shooting through the elevator shaft."[2]

Somehow Virginia forced her way out of the car into the sky lobby. She erupted in flames, her hair and blouse burning. She used her hands to put out the flames in her hair and then rolled on the ground to stop the burning on her body. When she finally sat back against the wall to rest, she saw that her hands and arms were completely burned. She didn't know that her face was badly burned too. She felt no pain. Two men helped her to the stairwell then walked ahead of her "so that they could catch her if she fell. She had to walk carefully because the burns on her hands kept her from holding onto the stair rail."[3] Virginia may have been one of the burn victims who passed by.

About the same time the burn victims are passing by us in the stairwell, another plane hits the South Tower, our sister tower. United Airlines Flight 175 from Boston crashed into Tower 2, lower this time, exploding into the sky lobby on the 78th floor. But in the concrete stairwell, it's as quiet as a cave. We keep moving, shuffling down the stairs, staying to the right so the injured can pass by on the left, but it's quiet up above. No more are coming. *It seems like more people should be coming down from the top floors. Where are they? There must be more injured.*

What I didn't know then is that the top of our building had become a death trap. Hundreds perished instantly when the plane crashed above us, and hundreds more on the floors above were blocked, unable to get out. We had kept the left side of the stairwell open for the injured, but most of them never made it down.

My throat is coated with the stench, like it's been painted in gasoline. I try to keep my breathing shallow. Then I hear a woman's voice. "I can't breathe," she says. She has stopped moving and sounds frightened. "I don't think we're going to make it out." She's somewhere close by. Her fear is palpable in the close atmosphere of the bodies in the stairwell. She's not in a full-blown panic, but she's close.

The line stops moving for a moment. People murmur encouragement and reassurance. Voices are gentle, concerned. No one lashes out in anger or frustration. We gather around her as a group. "It's going to be okay," several say. "We are going to make it."

I give her a hug. Without urging, Roselle nudges her hand, asking to be petted. A nudge from a Labrador retriever is more like a punch than a tickle, and the woman can't ignore it. She pets Roselle's head, stroking her soft fur. Roselle enjoys the attention and the break, panting happily. The woman relaxes, her breathing slows, and she even laughs a bit. Roselle has worked her magic.

The panicked woman takes a deep breath, gives Roselle one last pat, then takes her place in the line, heading downstairs once again.

I take a deep breath too. *Are we really going to make it? Maybe she's right, because it's getting harder to breathe.*

As we support and encourage each other in the stairwell, I think back to someone who was once a great source of encouragement to me.

805-947-8675. Mr. Herboldsheimer's phone number. I still remember it, and it's been years now.

Dick Herboldsheimer, or Mr. Herbo, as he liked to be called, was my geometry teacher in the ninth grade. He was a brilliant man, gifted in math, who had been working for the Kansas Nebraska Natural Gas Company and trying to support a wife and infant son on a whopping $1.65 an hour. He went back to school and earned both a BA and MA in mathematics. Lucky for me, he needed a better-paying job than they were offering him back in the Midwest, and he ended up teaching at Palmdale High School. His very first year teaching, he ended up with a blind kid in his geometry class. Me.

"It was like the principal dropped a bomb on me," said Mr. Herbo. "I had no idea of how I would cope." He was not only suffering from the shock of trading the lush, green fields of Nebraska for the hot, dry high desert, but now he had to figure out how to teach me a subject that is inherently visual. Geometry, one of the oldest sciences, is a branch of mathematics concerned with questions of size, shape, relative position of figures, and properties of space. The word *geometry* means "earth-measuring" in ancient Greek. But if I couldn't see shapes on a piece of paper, how on earth was Mr. Herbo going to teach me how to measure them?

The first day of class, I sat in the front row directly in front of his desk with my guide dog Squire. Mr. Herbo, probably nervous as could be, began to write out the first set of equations. "Mr. Herboldsheimer, you've got to tell me what you are writing on the blackboard," I said. He paused, thought for a minute, and then began to explain exactly what he was writing. And that was the beginning of a wonderful year.

I stayed in the front row. I had a Braille geometry book, and I took my geometry tests in the library with Mr. Herbo. We used an erasable slate, and Herbo used the stylus to draw images for me to use on the tests. He would take my finger and show me the raised image and then I would do the calculations and give him the answer orally.

"What great training that was for me as a new teacher. I think I learned as much or more from you than you learned from me," Mr. Herbo told me. "You could do calculations in your head faster than the kids in class could on paper."

On my birthday, Mr. Herbo invited me to Foster's Freeze for a banana split, and we made it an annual event. He was amazed when the servers couldn't tell I was blind. Even though my eyes are not functional, the structure of my eyes is intact, and so are the muscles that move my eyes and my eyelids. I have learned to look at people, using their voice and movements to cue in on their locations and heights, so when you talk to me, you will probably get the impression that I am looking at you, even though I have no vision. Blind people have eye colors that range the spectrum. My eyes are a light, milky color. I like to think they match my strawberry blond tresses.

One day I invited Mr. Herbo to my house to see my ham radio setup. My dad and I were licensed ham operators, and with our high-frequency radios we could talk to people on any part of the globe. My parents had given me a small room in the house to set up the equipment, and when Mr. Herbo came over, I took him back to show it off. I went in first and started booting up the system. I was busy and didn't notice that Mr. Herbo hung back.

"I can't see what you're doing," Mr. Herbo said. I was working in pitch black.

"Sorry, Mr. Herbo," I said. "I forgot you can see."

Mr. Herbo and I stayed in touch for many years. He came to my wedding and visited Karen and me several times. At one point we lost touch for a while. Finally Mr. Herbo looked up my number one day and gave me a call, out of the blue. When I picked up the phone, he said, "Hello, Mike."

"Hi, Mr. Herbo!" It had been fifteen years, but I will never forget his voice. I always end our conversations with, "Just remember, Mr. Herbo, I'll always be younger than you."

While many of my teachers were as encouraging and accommodating as Mr. Herbold-sheimer, my high school experience was not without obstacles. In the spring of my freshman year, I was called into the assistant principal's office. "We have a problem, Mike," he said. He opened up the Palmdale High School student handbook and began to read: "No live animals of any kind are allowed on school buses." I had been riding the bus to school with my very first guide dog, Squire. We were both still new and building our handler–guide dog relationship, but Squire was doing a great job. He minded his own business on the bus and had never caused any problems. The other kids were interested in him for the first few days, but after the novelty wore off, they went back to discussing kid stuff, and everything went back to normal. So I was shocked and confused. The law is clear. Certified guide dogs can legally go anywhere a blind person goes.

I went home and checked the handbook for myself. That I even had access to the handbook was due to the work of a wonderful local group called the Antelope Valley Braille Transcribers. At that time, not many Braille books were mass-produced, so many books and other printed materials had to be transcribed into Braille, page by page, by volunteers. Later on, in the late '60s, transcribed books began to be mass-produced using a thermoforming device. It was a slow process whereby the bumps on a Braille page were transferred to a special sheet of plastic. The plastic sheet was heated and then used to imprint a sheet of paper, resulting in a duplicate page of Braille. The process was something like a printing press, but it was revolutionary and meant that books and other printed materials could be produced cheaper and more quickly, a page at a time. But at this point, we didn't have access to this type of device and that meant most school-related materials had to be laboriously hand transcribed.

I pored over my hand-inscribed Braille student handbook and found the school bus rules. It was right there under my fingers. According to the handbook, Squire was not allowed on the bus.

Guide Dogs for the Blind had given me a special card to carry. It read, "California law guarantees a blind person the legal right to be accompanied by a specially trained dog guide in all public accommodations and on all public transportation." But the card wasn't any help now.

As irritated as my dad had been when the neighbors called to complain about the blind kid riding his bike, he was a hundred times more incensed now. He called the assistant principal that evening and asked if there had been a complaint about Squire. There had not. The school offered me alternate transportation; they planned on hiring a car and driver to take me to and from school. But this idea, besides costing the school district unnecessary expense, went against everything my parents had tried to do. My entire childhood was about finding a way for me to fit in and function in the community, not separating me and treating me as special or disabled.

My dad requested a special school board meeting to discuss the issue. Meanwhile, the district hired a private car and driver to ferry me back and forth to school. The Saturday before the school board meeting, my dad spent the day in the Palmdale Public Library, scouring *Black's Law Dictionary,* known as the most widely used law dictionary in the United States and the reference of choice for definitions in legal briefs and court opinions.

California law was clear: "Any blind person, deaf person, or disabled person who is a passenger on any common carrier, airplane, motor vehicle, railway train, motorbus, streetcar, boat, or any other public conveyance or mode of transportation operating within this state, shall be entitled to have with him or her a specially trained guide dog, signal dog, or service dog."[4]

The question my dad was researching was, is the school bus operated by the public school district considered a "public conveyance"? Dad reasoned that Palmdale High School was a public high school and all children in the district boundaries were allowed to attend. The school bus was a vehicle utilized by the school district to transport children to this public facility, so in his mind it qualified as a common carrier. My dad's library research bore out his assumption.

Mom, Dad, and I attended the meeting at the school district office in the public meeting room. It smelled like chalk dust, Old Spice, and Brylcreem. There were six or eight rows of chairs, and we sat in the front row. The school board members sat across the front of the room with the chairman in the middle. Squire rested quietly at my feet. I was nervous and excited.

The school board took several hours to work through its agenda while we waited for our item to come up. Mom left to have a smoke a couple of times, and Dad's foot tapped quickly, shaking the bench. Finally it was our turn.

The superintendent began with a pronouncement: "The Board of Education has set a rule that no live animal will be allowed on the school bus. As a board, we are tasked with enforcing the rules. We will not make an exception to the rule."

My dad stood up, facing the board, was recognized, and asked, "Did anybody complain?"

The superintendent answered no.

"Did my son or his guide dog misbehave?" No, again.

"The fact is, under California law it is a felony to deny access to public transportation to a blind person with a guide dog."

Go, Dad. I was proud.

"You can have all the rules you want, but you are violating the law." He was getting heated now. "If you guys keep this up, somebody's going to spend time in the penitentiary."

The superintendent was quiet. The atmosphere in the room was thick with tension. My dad's challenge lingered in the air. Then the superintendent turned to the chairman of the board who worked as a lawyer and asked, "Is that true?" His voice was laced with arrogance. The lawyer said yes, it was true.

Pause again. Then an answer. His voice was loud and clear. "Well, we have our rules, and we have to go by our rules. Our local rules supersede the law because it's a school situation." My dad pointed out that since the school district had hired a car and driver to ferry me to school, that made that car a school bus under the law. The board chose to ignore his arguments and voted 2 to 3 in favor of supporting the school board rule. We had lost. Squire and I had been officially kicked off the school bus. My parents fumed all the way home.

My dad was not yet done. His next step was a direct appeal to Edmund "Pat" Brown, the governor of California. Governor Brown was an advocate for progressive and populist causes, including education and fair housing, and his tenure was marked by social change. Dad wrote a letter to the governor explaining what had happened and requesting my reinstatement on the school bus. His plea was supported by a careful, detailed argument, the fruits of his library research. He ended the letter with "This is wrong. The school board is discriminating against my son."

Dad mailed his letter off to Sacramento.

Next thing we heard, the superintendent of the Antelope Valley School District was summoned to a meeting at the state capitol. He went. I wish I could have been a fly on the wall in that room.

A few days later I got called into the assistant principal's office once again. This time, the news was better. "Well, you're back on the school bus," the principal said. "Your dad made it happen." He clapped his hand on my shoulder. I smiled, big.

I was proud of my dad. Chalk one up for a man who never went beyond the eighth grade but who could wield a law dictionary when necessary. I learned that it is appropriate to take a stand and to defend a principle even if you have to knock on the governor's office door in the process. Sometimes the little guy wins.

High school went smoothly after that. I was pretty quiet and a bit of a nerd. Dad and I loved our ham radios and were part of the Civil Defense network called RACES, as well as the Military Affiliated Radio Service (MARS), the network of amateur radio operators who helped military personnel overseas communicate with loved ones here in the States. I kept busy with Boy Scouts, church choir, and academics. I joined the math club and became a mathlete, part of a mathematics team that participated in team competitions solving difficult math problems. I did all the work in my head and was pretty competitive.

I loved big band music, and my favorite

singing group was the Kingston Trio. I also loved musicals, and my cousin Rob and I drove our parents crazy singing the songs from *Music Man* at the top of our lungs in the car on a family trip to Yosemite. There was a lot of "Trouble in River City" on that trip.

Then I fell in love. Not with a girl, but with old radio shows. I loved Jack Benny and Fred Allen. Their quick and self-deprecating brand of humor tickled me. I listened to a military show called *Command Performance* featuring performers such as Bing Crosby, Bob Hope, Jimmy Durante, Frank Sinatra, Judy Garland, Dinah Shore, and the Andrews Sisters. The Beatles were just getting popular, but I loved the old stuff. I still do. I also listened to action shows like *Gunsmoke; Yours Truly, Johnny Dollar;* and *Have Gun, Will Travel.* When I got to college, I made some serious money through my love for old radio programs. My dad let me use his tape recorder to tape radio shows. I created a database of my collection and sold copies of old shows to collectors. I still enjoy them and have more than fifty thousand vintage radio shows in my collection. Decades later, the shows never grow old, and they never stop making me laugh. As Jack Benny would say, "Age is strictly a case of mind over matter. If you don't mind, it doesn't matter."

I was too busy with school and scouting to think much about girls yet, although my parents made me take dance lessons. I also learned how to play piano, but I wish my piano teacher had let me play by ear. I hated having to read music by Braille because you had to play one-handed while the other hand read the notes. Michael Blizzard Hingson did not like to slow down.

Even so, there are times when leaping out in front may not be the best choice. One day, many years later, a trip down the stairs would require a 100 percent team effort.

In the stairwell I start using an old trick the Boy Scouts taught me, checking the heat by touching the fire doors on each floor. I loved being a scout. I'm an Eagle Scout and a member of the Order of the Arrow, Scouting's honor society. Two million young men have earned the Eagle Scout designation, while only 180,000 have earned the right to don the Order of the Arrow sash, which recognizes cheerful service to others. Once an Eagle, always an Eagle.

Then, more panic. Overwhelmed by the burn victims, the smell of the jet fuel, and the overall terror, David Frank's voice begins to quiver. "Mike, we're going to die. We're not going to make it out of here."

My hand tightens for a moment on Roselle's harness. She looks up at me, I know, watching my face and listening for a command. I relax my hand. *I need to stay calm for Roselle. I cannot panic. I cannot let her sense any shred of fear in me.*

"David," I say quietly, so only he can hear. I use my best managerial voice. "If Roselle and I can go down the stairs, then so can you."

I'm not afraid of the fire. If those burned women can make it down the stairs, so can we. Roselle is quiet and calm next to me. I know if the fire had gotten close, she would have become nervous and pulled at her harness. I'm not afraid of the descent; people are working together to evacuate, and it won't be long before we're out of the building and on our way home.

But I am afraid of one thing. I can't banish this thought from my mind. It's there, nagging at me. A chill runs across my back. *What will I do if the lights go out?*

6
DRIVING IN THE DARK

A joke is a very serious thing.
WINSTON CHURCHILL

The stairwell is bathed in fluorescent light. Some of the fixtures give off a slight, comforting buzz as we continue down the stairs. I remember hearing that in the 1993 bombing at the World Trade Center, when a Ryder truck filled with 1,500 pounds of explosives was detonated in the garage of our building by a terrorist named Ramzi Yousef, people had to walk down darkened stairwells, and for some it took more than three or four hours to evacuate. *What would happen if the lights went out?* I keep pushing away the thought.

David, once right in front of me, has passed several people and moved about a floor ahead. He begins to act as scout, calling back whatever he sees. Every few floors, he calls back the number. "Sixty." Then

99

"Fifty-nine . . . fifty-six . . . fifty-four . . . fifty."

I'm still touching the fire doors, but they are cool. The fire must be contained to the upper floors although the air is still foul. There is a hint of smoke as well.

As the traffic in the stairwell continues to build, the atmosphere warms. Bodies are closer together. Adrenaline is pumping. The acrid smell of sweat hangs in the air. The railing under my right hand feels warm and damp now, losing its original cool metal feel to the dozens, maybe hundreds, of hands gripping it on the way down.

I'm still timing my breathing to the steps, but Roselle is breathing fast. Today our partnership is working well. While guide dog training has prepared Roselle to confront new and dangerous situations, there is no way any dog could ever be prepared for something like this. "Good girl," I say to Roselle. "You are doing a great job. I am so proud of you."

I give her head a quick rub, and she lifts her head up against my hand. I slide my hand down around her left ear and stroke her throat. It's damp. *I bet her body is trying to flush out the stench of the fumes. I hope it doesn't hurt her.*

"Forty-eight . . . forty-five . . . forty-three," David calls back. I touch my watch. It's 9:05. While our pace is slowing, my anxiety level begins to ratchet up. We're heading down the stairs at a steady pace. Roselle is doing her job. David is ahead, scouting. But the buzz of the lights brings the fear back. *What if the lights go out?*

As I walk, I mull over what I know so far. *There's been an explosion, and the building took a tremendous hit. The explosion rocked the building, blew out windows, and ignited a maelstrom of a fire. From the smell of the jet fuel, I'm pretty sure an airplane struck our building. So far, there has been no hint of emergency assistance. There are no alarms, no firefighters, and the fire sprinklers have not activated. I'm assuming the power at the top of the building has been cut off by the explosion, but on the 78th floor we still had power in our office, at least when we left. We still have power in the stairwell. But how long will it last?*

There are no windows in the stairwell. There are hundreds of us enclosed in cement and steel. We don't know what's going on above us or below us. We have no idea what's happening outside or even on the floors as we pass by. Without cell phones or contact with the outside, we are, all of us, in a blind descent.

Then the thought I've been pushing away returns. I can't ignore it anymore. *What if the power goes out?* If the fire spreads or the power systems begin to fail for some other reason related to the crash, the stairwell would be plunged into darkness. Through voices, breath, and movement, I can tell that the people around me are anxious, driven by a desire to get out of the building and into fresh air and freedom. There is no panic yet. New Yorkers are tough. But if everything goes dark, that could change. The irony is that if the power went out, Roselle and I would be fine. After living for fifty years in a world designed for the sighted, I've been forced to find ways to adapt and to cope. My parents' refusal to send me away to a home for the blind because I might become a burden prompted me instead to get creative, to learn how to survive, and to find and use the tools I need to make a life. A very good life.

There are certain advantages to being blind. I can save money on electricity. When I became proficient at reading Braille, I used to stay up till all hours reading in the dark. I like to think my parents never knew, but parents know everything, so they probably had a pretty good idea of what I was doing when I was supposed to be sleeping. I've developed a strong awareness of people's thoughts and feelings, gleaned from the sounds of their movements and their voices. I can't read their faces or look in their eyes, so I read everything else. I can't even really verbalize how I pick up on feelings and thoughts; it's intuition, honed by years of listening carefully. I learned to hear the coffee table, I learned to hear the driveways on my street, and I learned to hear people's emotions, too.

Try it out. If you are angry or irritated, the muscles in your face tighten up, especially around your mouth and lips, and the tone of your voice changes. It's sharp and short. On the other hand, if you are happy and relaxed, even smiling, your voice takes on a relaxed, open tone. It's the same with other emotions and mental states, such as sleepiness, sadness, guilt, fear, anxiety, enthusiasm, and love. I can hear them. Anyone can, if they pay attention.

The challenge of growing up blind also forced me to develop a boldness and a confidence as I faced new situations. And working with a partner helps.

Suddenly a thought hits me. Of course! Why didn't I think of it before?

I can be a guide.

If the lights go out, Roselle will guide me, and I'll guide the others. The lights might not work, but we can still get out. Roselle and I will lead the way.

Immediately, the fear lifts. I take a deep breath, hold it, and breathe out. *Relax.* We are still moving downward, a long line of people on a journey none of us wanted or anticipated. But we are in it together.

I call out, my voice loud and strong. "Don't anybody worry. Roselle and I are giving a half-price special to get you out of here if the lights go out." People around me laugh. The mood lightens, and we talk quietly as we walk.

I like to think that even in the most serious situations, I can find humor or some other way of relieving stress. I learned a lot about this in college.

Heading off to college challenged me to learn how to manage my fears. At first, being out on my own was daunting, as it is for any freshman. I had visited the University of California at Irvine with my parents before high school graduation, and we got the chance to meet with the chairman of the physics department. Everyone in the department was warm and welcoming and seemed to have no qualms about having a blind kid, so I applied and was accepted. My parents were over the moon; all of their hard work was paying off.

It must have been hard to let me go out on my own into the sighted world. But just as they'd let me shove off on my bicycle and brave the mean streets of Palmdale, they let me take off to the manicured, curving pathways of Irvine. There were a good many more people at UCI than in the whole city of Palmdale, but I was excited and looking forward to the academic challenge.

I did have Squire with me, though. But I also had learned to use a white cane, and I explored just about every pathway on the 1,500-acre campus, located in the coastal foothills of Orange County just south of Los Angeles and only five miles from the Pacific Ocean. Whenever I walked with a cane, I purposely took different routes to build a 3-D map in my head so I would never get lost. Once I learned the campus, I rode my bike or walked with Squire to get around.

I also took different routes whenever I walked with Squire. Guide Dogs for the Blind trains students to travel a variety of routes so that a dog does not get overly familiar with a particular routine. I had a friend who walked her phone bill to the phone company office every month. One day she took a walk in the same neighborhood but headed to the dry cleaner's instead. Her guide dog didn't know; he dragged her into the phone company, ignoring her commands and tugging on his harness because he thought he was supposed to take her there. Like us, dogs are creatures of habit and easily fall into a rut, so it's better to keep them guessing.

One interesting route I discovered was underground. A one-hundred-yard-long utility corridor ran underground from the computer science building to the engineering building. For some reason, the facilities people kept the tunnel access doors unlocked, so I got in the habit of using it as a shortcut, as did many others. I usually had Squire with me, and there were places I had to duck for pipes. Squire noted the hazards and learned to guide me around them. The tunnels were pretty busy at times; it was one of those poorly kept secrets that college students love to share, even before the days of easy information sharing via texting and Facebook. On weekends, though, the tunnel was deserted, and I used it to exercise my dog. I would stand at one end and throw a SuperBall as hard as I could. The dog would chase it, and depending on how fast he was that day, he might catch it in flight or he might just have to run all the way to the other end. Sometimes there would be someone else coming along the tunnel from the other side, and the poor student would get caught in the crossfire and get a little miffed. But what's a SuperBall-shaped bruise or two among friends?

I bought my first car as an Irvine student — a '64 Ford Mustang with a leaky transmission. Even driving became an adventure for me. I made friends with some of the campus police officers at University of California–Irvine, and they didn't make much of a fuss about me occasionally driving around campus in the evenings. My dad had let me drive a few times at home, and when I was six or seven years old, a friendly mailman named Mr. Judd had let me help drive the mail truck every once in a while. I couldn't make echolocation work for driving a car, so I had to have someone direct me. And I didn't have a driver's license, so that limited my driving options — usually I had someone else drive me while I directed from the front passenger seat. But I loved the Mustang, and sometimes we'd have a parade and drive around campus or drive in the parking lots and honk and wave at friends just to get a reaction.

While getting around at Irvine wasn't

much of a challenge, the academics were. I had more competition from the other students, who worked at a higher level than I was used to; the teachers didn't always describe what they were doing when they wrote on blackboards or overhead projectors; and sometimes I missed out on getting involved in discussion groups. Whether that was due to some shyness on my part or some uncomfortable feelings on the part of the other students, I'm not sure.

But one wonderful thing about college is that I had access to most of the books in Braille or via recordings. The books and materials I couldn't read were read to me by readers, typically other college students who became my eyes and read to me a few hours a week. I started to find my academic sweet spot, keeping up with a demanding course load and participating in group discussions, sometimes even shaping discussions.

Math courses were the hardest, especially if I didn't have the material. It wasn't easy for readers who weren't math or physics majors to convey the equations to me. So I spent lots of time with readers, trying to understand theorems. One professor, Dr. Naylor, at first didn't describe much of what he was doing in his lectures. I kept at him, asking questions and trying to understand. He was gracious about the whole thing. One day he called me on the phone and said, "Thank you for helping me get to the point where I am verbalizing more." For all the math students who came after me, I apologize right now if Dr. Naylor overexplained things. I take full responsibility.

I began to fall in love with physics. C. S. Lewis, the great writer and Christian thinker, once said, "The sweetest thing in all my life has been the longing . . . to find the place where all the beauty came from." My love for physics and math is also a quest for beauty and for understanding how the world works. I had always been interested in science, especially electricity and magnetism, probably because of my dad's influence. For as long as I can remember, I was particularly drawn to physical science. In my freshman year of high school, my science teacher noted my interest and arranged for me to attend the senior physics class for the entire last quarter of my freshman year. I always knew that I would major in physics.

The precision and complexity of the mathematical equations applied to the real world through the science of physics appealed to my sense of order and balance and helped satisfy my curiosity about how the world works. Mathematician Henri Poincaré put it this way: "The scientist does not study nature because it is useful; He studies it because he takes pleasure in it, and he takes pleasure in it because it is beautiful. If nature were not beautiful, it would not be worth knowing."[1]

My passion for physics coupled with a great deal of hard work paid off in college when I made the dean's list every quarter. But to make that happen, most of my first years at the university were spent in academic pursuits rather than a social life. I had friends, but my best friend was probably my guide dog. I still wasn't too interested in girls. Instead I filled my life with academics, reading, and vintage radio.

My social life began to take off after I started my own radio show on KUCI, the campus radio station. My show featured vintage radio programs from 6 to 9 p.m. every Sunday night. I competed with *60 Minutes,* and around the city of Irvine the KUCI Radio *Hall of Fame* show pushed Mike Wallace's face in the ratings dust. The radio station operated out of a small room in the physical sciences building. Our equipment was pretty primitive and we each produced our own show. I did research to provide some background and commentary for each vintage radio show I featured. Sometimes I conducted interviews or chatted with callers. I became very comfortable talking to people I didn't know, and I even began trying out jokes on the air, sort of a poor man's Dr. Demento. For a while I made it a point to memorize one joke or insult a day. Here's one I still remember: "How do you tell a male chromosome from a female chromosome? You take down their genes." Don't like that one? Okay, here's another. "Don't pitch your tent on a stove, because you can't build a home on the range." The jokes came in handy later when I went into sales. The better the insult, the more respect you get from the other salespeople. And I had good teachers — Abbott and Costello, Jack Benny, Fred Allen, and Milton Berle.

Whenever I could, I tried to put people at ease with my blindness, even using it for laughs if I could. One of my radio station buddies and fellow science geeks was Mat Kaplan. He had a show on Sunday nights right after mine. He's still in radio, hosting and producing *Planetary Radio,* which covers everything related to space travel. One time he scraped up a hundred dollars, a lot of money for starving college students in those days, and ordered a small helium-neon laser from Edmund Scientific, the wonderful old mail-order science and gadget supply house that is still around. Back in the '70s, lasers were not yet widely available at every local drugstore like they are now. Mat and I had a great time playing with the laser, and we immediately noticed how my guide dog Holland was mesmerized by the bright laser pinpoint light and loved to chase it. We sent him into a frenzy chasing the laser around a big room by the radio station. The laser was so powerful, though, that we had to be careful. We didn't want to injure the dog's eyes by accident. But my eyes — that was a different story. Without giving Mat any warning, one time I picked up the laser and flashed the beam straight into my eye.

"Funny, I don't see anything," I dead-panned.

"Mike, Mike, don't do that!" yelled Mat, frantic. I think that was the last time he let me play with the laser.

Although desktop and laptop computers were still far in the future, UC Irvine had a mainframe computer. In the '60s, most mainframes accepted input from system operators via punched cards, paper or magnetic tape, or Teletype devices, which looked something like an IBM Selectric typewriter or the bulky old printers you used to see in newsrooms. By the '70s, at universities like Irvine, mainframes had interactive user interfaces and operated as time-sharing computers "talking" to many individual users as well as doing batch processing.

These were exciting times for physics students, as we were required to do extremely complex mathematical equations. The school computer could do calculations in a few seconds that would take us hours, and we were only at the beginning of understanding how computers could be used in the world outside the university walls.

But there was a problem. I couldn't use the computer even though I knew how to type. The Teletype had a standard QWERTY keyboard, but there was no way for me to read the display on the screen or decipher the output when it was printed out. I was virtually locked out of the computer age. I needed some help. John Halverson, another blind student a year ahead of me, also wanted access, so together we appealed to the powers that be for some technology to allow us to use the computer.

Enter Dick Rubinstein, a wunderkind graduate student and researcher at UCI working with Julian Feldman, head of the computer science program. Julian asked Dick to help us, and we immediately hit it off. It was an era when many college students were taking up political activism and making their voices heard, and John and I were no different. We came up with a phrase for our computer-access lobbying project. We took the popular slogan "Power to the People" and gave it a twist: "Blind Power." We had a great time joking around about our own civil rights movement, and Dick joined right in.

Then he got to work and whipped up a Braille terminal for us. Dick was an engineer who describes himself as "a generalist." He had just graduated from Caltech in engineering but had shifted gears at Irvine to study social sciences. Dick loves to make and fix things and has an innate understanding of how equipment works. He also loves people, and his sense of design comes from an understanding of what people need. He started with a Teletype machine that printed with a type cylinder that rotated and pressed against a ribbon to make marks on paper. It printed at only ten characters a second, very slow. Dick designed a new cylinder and installed pins to emboss the dots needed to create Braille marks along with a number of other modifications needed to put the paper in the right position to receive the marks. Then he wrote a software program to run on a Digital PDP-8 minicomputer to translate the received information into the Braille marks. The minicomputer acted as a controller for the Braille terminal.

"It wasn't fast, but it did the job," said Dick, who went on to earn his PhD and spend his career as a human factors engineer. His project was written up and published in 1972 in a journal for the Association for Computing Machinery.

Dick and I kept in touch and batted some ideas around on other sorts of Braille displays, and Dick went on to be involved in developing electronic mail (or *e-mail,* as we call it now) as a communications aid for deaf adults, way back in the late '70s when most people had never heard of e-mail yet and the Internet was still called the ARPA-NET. Smart guy. He loved my pachinko machine.

The pachinko was a mechanical Japanese gaming device that was similar to a vertical pinball machine. You shot small balls up into the machine, which then cascaded down through a mass of metal pins, sometimes landing in special pockets for bonus points.

"What's a blind guy doing with a pinball machine?" Dick once said.

"Wait until you see me play darts," I replied.

Dick's Braille terminal helped ignite my love affair with technology, and one of my passions is helping to put the latest, most powerful, and most easy-to-use technology in the hands of blind people. The technology we have available today has changed the rules of the game and given me and other blind people more independence and access to information than ever before. It's an exciting time to be blind.

When I graduated from UC Irvine with highest honors, my parents and my brother were in the audience, watching. Besides my brother, I was the first one in the whole family to earn a college degree. Well, besides Squire, my aging guide dog. Chancellor Aldrich awarded Squire a degree too. Only instead of physics, his degree was in "Lethargic Guidance," a nod to his propensity for frequent naps now that he was in his sunset years.

I stayed on at Irvine and earned a master's degree and a teaching credential. I also took some business courses that I thought might be useful out in the real world. But I did run into one roadblock at school. As I began to consider pursuing a doctorate degree in physics, I ran into some pushback, from certain professors, that seemed to be related to my blindness. I did some work with a lawyer and in the process gained access to my file in the physics department. We discovered a shocking letter. It read, "A blind person cannot do the high level work necessary for an advanced degree in physics."

At first I was stunned. Then I got angry. But those feelings passed pretty quickly, and I was left with a two-word response.

Why not?

As it happened, I ended up landing a great job right out of grad school, so I decided not to pursue a doctorate. But, I also decided to live out the rest of my life on the "why not" principle.

And those two words are my secret, the secret behind blind power. Why not? Why not ride a bike or drive a car or play darts or earn a PhD in physics? Why not try it all, just to see if I can do it?

Here's a great Milton Berle quote from my vintage radio show vault. He sums it up perfectly: "I'd rather be a could-be if I cannot be an are; because a could-be is a maybe who is reaching for a star. I'd rather be a has-been than a might-have-been, by far;

for a might-have-been has never been, but a has was once an are."

I think there is truth to the observation that your life passes before you when you face death or a very stressful situation and so I remembered my college life as I descended the stairs on September 11, 2001. I constantly looked for memories that could help me survive whatever happened to Roselle and me in our time of terror.

The temperature inside the stairwell continues to climb. I'm feeling more upbeat, so I try another joke. "All this walking is a great way to lose weight." Laughter again. Other quips filter back up to me. Each one puts a smile on my face.

Boy, do I need to lose some pounds, someone says.

I'm going to have a double dessert tonight! Laughter.

I never want to see another stairwell again as long as I live. We all agree.

For a moment, people sound almost lighthearted. Almost.

I chime back in. "I have an idea. On our first day back in the tower, let's all meet on the 78th floor at 8:45 a.m. and walk down the stairs as a way to lose weight."

We've gone from being strangers to teammates. Somehow our fear and anxiety have turned into closeness and teamwork. The usual boundaries are down. All we have is each other. We know instinctively that we must all work together to prevent panic, or we might not make it out.

Ten stairs, turn, nine stairs. "Thirty-nine . . . thirty-six . . . thirty-four," calls out David.

If the lights go out, Roselle and I are ready.

Then from somewhere on the flights below, I hear a murmur. There's something happening down below, and a ripple of tension and excitement makes its way up the line.

The firefighters are coming.

7
WARRIORS WITH GUIDE DOGS

Intuition is linear; our imaginations are weak. Even the brightest of us only extrapolate from what we know now; for the most part, we're afraid to really stretch.

RAYMOND KURZWEIL

Roselle's big Labrador tongue lolls down one side. The stairwell is hot, and we're walking down sometimes two abreast, sometimes single file, and beginning to pack more closely together. Since the explosion we've made it down to the 33rd floor.

I hear an excited buzz in the voices of the people below me, and I can just make out the words: "Water bottles!" Someone has broken open a vending machine, and people are passing cold water bottles up the stairs.

I pass a few bottles to the people behind me then twist open a bottle and take a few swallows. The cold water is a relief, and it tastes sweet compared to the acrid taste of the fumes.

Roselle nudges my hand. Her nose feels hot, and I wonder if she can smell the water. I bend over and offer her the bottle. She begins to lick the top, and I tilt it just a bit so she can drink the rest. I know she must be thirsty because she hasn't had anything to drink for a while. Many guide dogs don't eat or drink anything in the mornings so they don't have to interrupt work to relieve themselves, and Roselle is no different. She hasn't had any food or water since last night. She finishes up the bottle and wants more. She licks the last few drops. I can hear her smacking her lips, and then she begins to pant again. She's still thirsty.

"Good Roselle," I say. I gently grab the sides of her head, just under her ears. I rub her cheeks with my thumbs. Other people around me have stopped to drink some water, too, and I can feel them listening. "Good dog. You're doing great. Just keep going. You can do it."

I know I have to stay calm for Roselle. If I show fear or begin to panic, she will pick up on it and might get scared too. It's important that Roselle doesn't sense that I am afraid. If that happened, it would make it harder for us to get out. So far, we are staying calm and focused, and I'm able to control my fear.

But there is undercover fear all around us, the general panic level increasing the lower we go. I can hear it in the whispers, feel tension in the footsteps echoing around me. But Roselle does not react; she is in the moment, secure in herself and her work.

As long as the harness is on, even in a life-and-death situation, I am confident that Roselle will continue to do her job just as she always does. Besides the jet fuel, she can also smell the fear around us. When people are afraid, their autonomic nervous systems react with an increase in sweat gland activity, with the apocrine glands producing secretions through the hair follicles that result in a very faint odor that dogs are able to pick up. They don't exactly smell the emotion of fear, but they can smell the result: an olfactory fear signal inadvertently produced by the body. Dogs are not as visual as people, and their primary sense is smell, said to be a thousand times more sensitive than that of humans. Roselle has more than 200 million olfactory receptors in her nose, while I only have about 5 million.[1] These receptors feed information to the highly developed olfactory lobe in Roselle's brain, making her a scent machine.

She lives in a world of smell, not sight, and thus is not light-dependent, either. We have that in common.

She has her ears too; dogs can hear sound at four times the distance humans can. That means if I can hear things happening twenty steps below, she can clearly hear what's going on eighty steps below. She also has a powerful sense of touch. Not only does she hone in on the signals I send through my hand on the upright handle of her harness, but her entire body is covered with touch-sensitive nerve endings, and around her eyes, muzzle, and jaws, she has exquisitely sensitive hairs called *vibrissae* that continuously feed her information about her environment.

On top of that, dogs seem to have a sixth sense, sometimes surprising us by predicting earthquakes or finding their way home from a distant location. They can read our moods through our pheromones, the chemicals produced by our bodies in connection with emotion. They seem sensitive to changes in the earth's magnetic field and to infrared wavelengths of light. And, like Roselle did earlier this morning, dogs can detect sudden changes in barometric pressure, like when a storm is brewing.

Thinking about Roselle's special abilities

123

gives me confidence. *We are going to make it out.* My teamwork with Roselle and the confidence it gives each of us seem to transmit to the people immediately around us, almost like a zone of security. We are close on the stairwell and our defenses are down. All we have is each other, and there is a feeling of working together to make it out safely. We are strong.

A few steps below, David calls out. "There are firemen coming up the stairs. Everyone move to the side." I go down to where David stands.

It's the 30th floor, and here they come. As they approach, we instinctively string out into a single-file line to let them pass. The firefighters are loaded down with equipment. Besides having to wear protective thigh-length jacket and pants, most of them carry fifty or sixty pounds of gear, including helmets, gloves, axes, and air tanks. They are tired and sweaty, and they're not even halfway up to the fire.

Later, reports on the events of September 11 would suggest that the firefighters in the stairwell didn't know much more about what was going on than we did. Cell phones and radios weren't working well and communication was spotty at best. Oral histories from the few firefighters who survived say they were "clueless" about the details and knew "absolutely nothing" about the reality of the impending crisis.[2]

"Hey, buddy. Are you okay?" The very first of a long line of firefighters stops and talks to me on the 30th floor.

"I'm fine." I feel Roselle moving and I know he is petting her. It doesn't seem like the time to give him a lecture about not petting a guide dog in harness.

"We're going to send somebody down the stairs with you."

"You don't have to do that. Things are going fine and I don't think I need help."

"Well, we're going to send somebody down with you, because we want to make sure you get down okay."

I think of the millions of pieces of burning paper raining down outside my office windows. *These guys need to get up those stairs to fight the fire.*

"You don't have to do that." I can tell he's determined to help me. "I've got a guide dog and we're good."

"Nice dog," he says, stroking Roselle. She is friendly, as usual, and gently mouths his hand.

"Anyway, you can't get lost going downstairs." I try to make it light.

His voice deepens and takes on a bit of an edge. I can tell he's used to being listened to. "We're going to send somebody with you."

I want to tell him my blindness isn't a handicap, but it's not the right time for that lecture either. I use the last gun in my arsenal. "Look, my friend David is here. He can see, and we're fine."

The firefighter turns to David. "Are you with him? Is everything okay?" David reassures him we're fine.

I hear him shrug his shoulders and resettle the tank on his back, and I know he's about to head upstairs. The men below him stir, restless. They're anxious to get upstairs and get to it.

"Is there anything we can do to help you guys?" I ask.

"No," he says. "You've got to go."

He gives Roselle one last pat. She kisses his hand and then he is gone. I would realize later that this touch was probably the last unconditional love he ever got.

I tighten my grip on the harness. The cold water is long gone, and I can taste the jet fuel again.

"Forward." We head down the stairs. I think about Roselle and the firefighter and wonder, *Can she smell courage?*

I've had a lifetime to develop the skills needed to navigate through a world not set up for me. And if there's one thing I've learned, it's this: sight is not the only game in town.

Blindness is not a handicap; it's something I've always lived with. The real handicap comes from the prejudices people have about blindness. I knew the firefighter was only trying to help, but sometimes help is not what I need. Even so, the firefighter couldn't be diverted until I pointed out that I had a sighted colleague "assisting me."

I just use a few different tools than other people do. One of the tools I got along the way allowed me to do something I've always wanted to do: pilot an airplane. But first let me tell you about some of the others.

It all started with Braille, my entry into the world of words and ideas. Unfortunately, the majority of blind people cannot read Braille. A tactile system developed in Paris by Louis Braille in 1821, Braille is a reading and writing language all blind people should learn how to use. By using combinations of up to six raised dots, a person can interpret printed codes for letters of the alphabet or combinations of letters by running an index finger across the raised surfaces.

In fourth grade, my parents bought me a Braille writer from Germany, called a Marburg. A Braille writer is a wood-and-metal machine about half the size of a typewriter. Six Braille keys and a spacing key are made of wood topped with ivory. The six keys operate the mechanism that produces dots to form the letters, contractions, or symbols used to write Braille. Paper is fed into a cylindrical paper roller and turning knobs at either end of the roller feeds the paper into the machine.

The Perkins Brailler, manufactured by Perkins Products/Howe Press in Massachusetts, was the best Braille writer on the market, but it cost more than a hundred dollars, a small fortune at the time. The Marburg was half that, so I used it for three years before the local Lions club bought me a Perkins.

When I was nine, I discovered "talking books" and became enthralled with Perry Mason, the defense attorney determined to prove his clients' innocence, and Nero Wolf, the fat, gourmet private detective. I listened to many classic and contemporary books recorded on twelve-inch records. These books were created by a program administered by the Library of Congress. Special libraries were established throughout the United States to distribute or loan out these books to blind people. Some books required ten to twenty records, and I remember hearing that the recording of *The Rise and Fall of the Third Reich* required fifty-six records. I decided to skip that one.

I still listen to talking books, work on my computer, and use Braille daily. But instead of a wood, metal, and ivory manual Braille writer, I now use a BrailleNote, a small computer about the size of a medium size hardcover book with a tactile display that allows me to electronically read and write in Braille with no monitor needed.

Another technological tool I use daily is a talking smart phone. I have software on my computer that operates a screen reader that verbalizes the information contained in documents, spreadsheets, and on Web sites. After years of practice, I can listen to and decipher the voice of my screen reader at hundreds of words a minute. The voice sounds a little like an auctioneer on speed, but it allows me to get through e-mail and documents quickly.

Just a couple of years ago, along came a game changer that enabled me to do something I never thought I'd be able to do — read my mail. Think about it. For a blind person to read mail, he has to ask a friend or hire an assistant to help read it. But now, thanks to the K-NFB Reader by Mobile Products, I can read any sort of print, whether menus, magazines, instructions, labels, recipes, or even junk mail. It works like this: using a cell phone, the user takes a photo of the print to be read and the character recognition software, in conjunction with high-quality text-to-speech, reads the contents of the document aloud.

The K-NFB Reader is the great-grandchild of the Kurzweil Reading Machine, the world's very first omni-font optical character recognition system. This remarkable machine was invented by Raymond Kurzweil, a futurist and inventor who came up with a computer program capable of recognizing text written in any font. Before that time, scanners had only been able to read text written in a very few standardized fonts.

Kurzweil had known he wanted to be an inventor since the age of six. While a student at MIT, he became interested in using computers for pattern recognition. His ideas were innovative but needed a real-world application.

One day Kurzweil was on an airplane and struck up a conversation with a blind man sitting next to him. He asked what type of technology would be most helpful in addressing a blind person's needs. He expected the answer to be related to mobility. Instead, the man said the technology that would be the most helpful would be a device that could read print.

After that chance conversation, Kurzweil decided that the best application of his scanning technology would be to create a reading machine that would allow blind people to understand written text by having a computer read it to them aloud.

My very first job out of college, in a remarkable stroke of luck, I got to work with Raymond "Ray" Kurzweil, now an internationally recognized inventor and futurist.

Ray first approached the National Federation of the Blind (NFB) with his idea for a reading machine back in 1974. They were skeptical at first, but after an eye-opening demonstration at the inventor's laboratory on Rogers Road in Massachusetts where the reading machine read some of the materials the NFB brought, they began a working relationship. With Ray's help, the NFB approached foundations for funding and purchased five machines, which were placed in various locations around the country for blind people to use. These were the prototypes and were about the size of an apartment-sized washing machine. The reading machine used a flatbed scanner and scanned just one line at a time. It took about thirty to forty-five seconds to scan an 8 1/2 × 11–inch page of text, then another minute or so to recognize the text and begin to read it out loud.

The first five machines were located at the Iowa Commission for the Blind; Blind Industries and Services of Maryland; the New York Public Library; the University of Colorado; and the Orientation Center for the Blind in Albany, California (later moved to the San Francisco Public Library).

These machines were just prototypes and needed the bugs worked out, so after graduation I was hired by the NFB to work with James Gashel, director of governmental affairs for the NFB, to test the machines out in the real world. It was my job to teach people how to use them and to write the training curriculum. I traveled from place to place, collecting data about how people were using the machines, and then incorporated that into recommendations for the production model of the machines. I was the day-to-day guy. I had a ball traveling around the country, teaching people how to use the machines and helping to make their experience a good one so they could use the machines and provide us with feedback. My findings helped refine the design and make it more user-friendly. I even helped come up with the concept of a "nominator" key, which directed the machine to read aloud the names and functions of the control keys. We also came up with a "Contrast" control to make light print appear darker to the camera, thus widening the amount of material those first machines could read.

In 1978, I began to work directly for Ray at Kurzweil Computer Products. I ended up doing the same thing I had done before, working on human-factor studies and coming up with ways to make the machine better and even more user-friendly. Later I ended up moving into the sales force and selling the commercial version of the product. I took a Dale Carnegie sales course and helped to move the reading machine into the corporate world, where it was a great product for companies who wanted to scan documents. Eventually Xerox purchased Kurzweil's company in order to get at the scanner technology and brought in their own people. I was the last non-Xerox person to be laid off from the sales force.

During my time in Boston, I became

friends with Aaron Kleiner, who had been Ray's roommate at MIT and who worked closely with Ray. Once I talked Aaron into going with me to see the first Star Wars movie. It was a very big deal and lines were long. He couldn't believe a blind guy wanted to go to the movies. He thought it was even more hilarious when I asked him to describe the visuals. "That was a challenge," Aaron said. "I'll never forget trying to describe the cantina scene. 'Uh, there's a guy with the head of a grasshopper and the body of a horse . . .'"

Aaron and I had an even more interesting experience at a ritzy restaurant in Boston's Back Bay. There were three of us: Aaron, his wife, and me. The minute we walked in the front door, the maître d' took one look at my guide dog, Holland, and said, "We're sorry. We don't allow dogs. You can't come in here." I wasn't too upset; since I'd dealt with this before.

"This is wrong," I said. "They don't know the law."

We left and had dinner at a different restaurant, but Aaron's wife was shaking, she was so angry. I told her, "Don't worry. I know what to do."

The next day, I printed out a copy of the guide dog law and contacted the local chapter of the National Federation of the Blind. I rounded up six or seven other blind people with guide dogs, and we showed up for dinner back at the restaurant with the snooty maître d'. We opened the door and surged in, a pack of blind warriors with our trusty dogs.

The maître d' stopped. Looked at us. Blinked. Considered his options. Caved.

"Welcome," he said.

We had a wonderful dinner and were treated well. The restaurant staff was solicitous, even offering food to the guide dogs.

Blind power.

The Kurzweil Reading Machine was revolutionary. On January 13, 1976, the finished product was rolled out by Raymond Kurzweil and NFB during a news conference. It gained him national recognition. On the day of the machine's unveiling, Walter Cronkite used the machine to give his signature send-off, "And that's the way it is, January 13, 1976." While listening to the *Today* show, musician Stevie Wonder heard a demonstration of the device and purchased the first production version of the Kurzweil Reading Machine, beginning a lifelong friendship with Ray. Ray was later inducted into the National Inventors Hall of Fame for this invention. He was also awarded the National

Medal of Technology by President Bill Clinton for pioneering new technologies.

Ray was always interested in music and went on to start a company that developed the most state-of-the-art music synthesizer in the industry. He ended up selling that company to Yamaha. Later he started working on voice recognition, and the most successful programs currently on the market are based on algorithms he created.

That washing machine–sized reading machine that originally cost fifty thousand dollars is now under two thousand bucks, and I carry the software on my cell phone so I can use it to read anything, anywhere, anytime.

Oh, and one last tool. This is the one that allowed me to fly a plane. Not long ago I purchased a GPS system that integrated with my Braille Notetaker. This system was developed by another blind man, Mike May, and his company, the Sendero Group. I had to fly to a speaking engagement in Idaho. My brother-in-law Gary Ashurst had arranged for me to deliver a speech in Hailey, Idaho, and he also arranged for a friend to come to Boise to fetch me in his private plane.

It was a clear and beautiful autumn day. While we were walking to his four-seater

Cessna, the pilot noticed my BrailleNote hanging over my shoulder. He also examined my new GPS receiver and started asking questions. Before we took off, I showed him how it worked and told him I was going to use it to track our flight.

I got Roselle settled in, I buckled up, and we took off.

Just after we lifted off the runway, the pilot asked me a question I never thought I would hear. "How would you like to fly the plane to Hailey?"

I didn't need a second invitation. After all, if I could learn to hear a coffee table, ride my bike around Palmdale, hop on a horse, play golf, and drive a car around the UC Irvine campus, then I could certainly fly a plane.

Since I was sitting in the right-hand seat, which also contained full access to the equipment necessary to fly the plane, I took the controls. I got some instructions on how to use the stick and other relevant controls, and then the pilot released the operations to me. My trusty GPS talked me through the skies above Idaho and guided me to the Hailey airport in about an hour. Roselle snored through the whole thing.

I was able to land the plane with a few instructions. In the process, we noticed the altimeter on the GPS was not quite accurate. In fact, it was one hundred feet off, showing that we were lower than we actually were. It didn't ruffle me much; I'd rather err on the low side than think the plane was higher than it really was.

For blind people, emerging technology is changing the rules of the game, and the sky's the limit.

8
I Forgot You Are Blind

"Prejudice comes from being in the dark;
sunlight disinfects it."

MUHAMMAD ALI

Firefighters continue to stream up the stairs.
Almost every single one stops to look at me,
Roselle, and David. Over and over the same
few words. "Are you okay?"

"I'm just fine. Thank you," I say.

"Are you with him?" they ask David.

"Yes, I'm with him. We're fine. Thanks."

As the firefighters pass, sometimes sponta-
neous clapping breaks out. I hear people
thanking them and patting their shoulders.
They're breathing heavily.

Progress is slow now. The closer we get to
the bottom, the faster, not slower, I want to
go.

People are always surprised at how fast I
walk. It's different, of course, when I'm

139

exploring a place for the first time. I usually leave my guide dog at home and use my white cane as an extension of my hands, and as it swings back and forth, tapping the ground, walls, and any objects in my path, I use it almost like a surveying device. It becomes a probe, and I use the information it conveys to map out a graphic, three-dimensional, detailed representation of the new location. I did this with the World Trade Center when I first started working there, exploring top to bottom until I knew it as well as I knew the cracks in the sidewalk in Palmdale.

Most people think the cane is just a tool to use to detect obstacles in your walking path, but it's much more. Tapping the cane creates sounds unique to the terrain. Dirt, stone, cement, asphalt, tile, wood, and rubber each create a unique sound that an experienced cane traveler learns to detect and identify. But the cane taps also generate an echo that good cane travelers learn to decode for information on the geography of the surrounding space just as I did years ago by listening to my bicycle tires as I rode around my neighborhood in Palmdale. For example, if I'm walking in a parking lot, the sound of the tap changes if there is a parked car in front of me before I ever get close enough to actually contact the car with my cane. As I walk through the cars, the tap sounds change again as I near the curb, the sound waves bouncing off the six inches of cement to create a unique echo. Over time I've learned to gather extensive information about my environment from the taps.

Human echolocation, as it is sometimes called, also works with finger snaps, light foot stomps, or clicking noises made with the mouth. While it's similar to the sonar and echolocation used by animals, humans make sounds with much lower frequencies and slower rates than bats and dolphins, so echolocation works for us mainly on larger objects. In other words, I can't locate and dispatch a pesky mosquito via mouth clicks or cane taps. I'll have to leave that to the bats. But human echolocation works well enough for a blind man named Daniel Kish to train people how to use the skill for activities such as mountain biking. Another man named Ben Underwood has used echolocation for running, Rollerblading, basketball, and skateboarding.

Since I've been using a cane since my teens, I walk pretty quickly. I like to use a long cane so I can extend it out about three feet in front of me.

With Roselle I can move just as fast except

that she handles the job of avoiding objects, helping me travel more efficiently because she makes the choices of how to best avoid obstacles. Roselle studies me constantly, matching my speed. More than once I've jogged down an airport concourse to catch a plane, probably turning a few heads. Roselle can usually keep up.

The slow pace on the stairs is frustrating, although understandable. Between the firefighters now taking up the left side of the stairs as they climb up, and the increasing size of the crowd in the stairwell, we are creeping along now. "Twenty-eight . . . twenty-five . . . twenty-two . . . ," David says.

On the 20th floor now, the floor feels slippery. *Why? What is it from? Spilled water? Sprinklers? Sweat?* No one says anything, so it must be some sort of clear liquid. I'm guessing water. But whatever the liquid is, it makes my job harder. I focus, gripping the stair railing a little tighter. I'm even more careful with my feet. Roselle's movements and pace aren't changing; she doesn't seem to notice the slippery stairs. But I need to be aware of her every move in case she slips, or in case I need to move quickly, increasing my chance of slipping.

"Eighteen . . . fifteen . . . thirteen . . ." I try to control my breathing. Roselle's breaths are coming fast. *Will we pass out from inhaling the fumes?*

I check my watch. It's 9:35 a.m. It took us just twenty minutes to travel from the 78th floor down to the 30th. But after we met the firefighters, progress was slower, and now we are down to a crawl. But we're getting close.

"Ten . . . nine . . . eight . . . seven . . . six . . ." Now I want out of the stairwell. I'm tired of counting. My legs are starting to feel wobbly. I want fresh air. I want to call Karen.

"Five . . . four . . . three . . . two . . ." We are so close. If I weren't hemmed in by people, I'd run.

"First floor," David calls back. "The sprinklers are on, and we're going to have to run through a waterfall at the bottom of the stairs."

He's not joking. Seconds later, when we reach the 1st floor and leave the stairs, I hear the sprinklers vibrating and water gushing onto the tile floor of the lobby. Roselle pulls down and dips her head to drink water off the floor. I know she's parched.

Wait! What's in that water? With the smell of the jet fuel still strong in my nose and

143

throat, I'm afraid the water might be contaminated. I hate to do it, but I pull firmly up on Roselle's harness to stop her.

"Hop up!" She responds, gracious as always, and looks up at me. I pause for a split second, the waterfall directly ahead. Then I take a big gulp of air. It's time to run.

"Forward!"

A torrent of water floods over me. It is colder and more powerful than any shower I've ever known. After the heat and the fumes of the stairwell, it feels like a baptism, a cool and revitalizing initiation back into the land of the living.

We made it. We're out.

I almost can't believe it.

"Good girl, Roselle. You did a great job." We're in the lobby of Tower 1 now, and I take a few moments to rub Roselle's head and stroke the back of her neck. She rubs her cheeks against my hand then pulls away and shakes, starting with her head. I drop the harness, keeping the leash in my left hand.

"Good girl," I say again. "Shake it off." I know what's coming next. I hear her ears flap back and forth; then, as any good canine shake does, it proceeds down her spine and ripples out her tailbone as she shakes off the water. Fine droplets spray my hands.

"Great job, Roselle. Good dog. Good girl." I pick up her harness. It's time to go home.

David approaches. "Let's go," he says. The lobby is in chaos, with people everywhere walking and running across the wet tile floor. It's a war zone. Ankle-deep water is full of debris, including ceiling tiles, building materials, and paper. Emergency workers are shouting, directing people towards the doors. Voices are anxious, strained, tight. A man approaches and identifies himself as FBI.

"Come this way," he orders.

"Where do you want us to go?"

He directs us toward the revolving doors to the underground central shopping arcade.

"Thank you," I call back as we walk away. "I appreciate your help." In the middle of a little piece of hell on earth, when all of his instincts must be screaming at him to leave, get out, run away and don't dare look back, this man stays put and offers his help. He is but one of many.

When I escaped Tower 1 that day, I had no idea it would be the last time I ever set foot inside the building. It's funny; when I talk about my 9/11 experiences today, people sometimes assume that I was there visiting, perhaps as a tourist. "What were you doing up on the 78th floor?" they ask. I can detect a faint sense of surprise when they begin to understand I was at work that day, just like thousands of other people.

But sometimes, when I think about it, I am surprised too. The unemployment rate for blind people is staggering, somewhere near 70 percent of employable blind people, according to the Social Security Administration. The reason that many of the blind unemployed cannot find jobs is that they have faced outright rejection because they are blind or because they have been discouraged by the fruitlessness of their attempts to find a job.

I understand. I once had a job interview scheduled in San Jose, California, for a company that was producing new voice technology products. The night before I was to fly upstate, the headhunter doing the coordination called. "I notice that you've worked with several blindness-oriented organizations like the National Federation of the Blind," he said.

"Yes, that's correct." I knew where this was leading.

"Is someone in your family blind?"

"No. I am blind."

Early the next morning, the interview was canceled.

My friend Dr. James Nyman, a former director of Nebraska Services for the Blind, faced a similar scenario when he first started out in the job market, seeking employment as a college teacher. He recalled "at least two rejection letters that flatly stated that a blind person could not manage the responsibilities of a faculty member." He believes attitudes have improved over the years, but the prejudice is still there, just under cover. "We are not likely to encounter such open declarations in today's atmosphere of social consciousness, but the more subtle forms are probably more difficult to combat," he said.[1]

Blind people face unnecessary barriers, and we can do far more than people think. But I have also learned that instead of thinking of blindness as a disability or a limitation, I can view it as a help. In fact, in my sales career my blindness became one heck of an asset.

First, I don't think of myself as "blind Michael Hingson." There are other descriptors that rank much higher. I am also a husband, friend, son, brother, cousin, dog owner, sales manager, physics grad, vintage radio show enthusiast, writer, speaker, networker, barbecue chef, ice cream maker, humorist, book lover, horseback rider, man of prayer, technology geek, pianist, world traveler, and dancer. And that's just for starters. Blind man is in there somewhere, but far down the list. One of the greatest compliments I get is when someone says, "I forgot you are blind." Then I know for sure that individual is relating to me as a multifaceted person, not through the lens of my blindness.

My brother, Ellery, reminded me recently of my very first meeting with his wife, Gloria. The two of them rode the train to meet me in Boston. Being a typical guy, Ellery didn't think to tell her much about me. I was just his brother, Mike. I was single at the time, and I met Ellery and Gloria at the train station and led them to a cab. It was about four thirty in the afternoon, and traffic was slow. I directed the cabbie to take some shortcuts back to my apartment, and we skirted some of the congestion. At my apartment after we chatted a bit, I made a lobster dinner for the three of us. It was delicious. We made it almost the whole evening before Gloria noticed I was blind. That was delicious, too — just three people having a wonderful dinner and enjoying

148

each other's company.

After my stint at Kurzweil Computer Products was over, I looked for something else in the high-tech arena. I enjoyed the challenge of sales and working together with customers to determine their needs. In the mid-1980s I started my own company with a friend selling specialized computer systems, including some of the early computer-aided design (CAD) systems that architects use. We did okay but didn't make a lot of money. It may seem strange that a blind person could sell CAD systems until you think about it. When architects who came to see our products asked for demonstrations, I would sit them down in front of the screen and ask them what they wanted to draw and how they would do the job on their drafting tables. I then took them through the steps of drawing on a CAD system so that by the end of the demonstration, they had drawn their own building and could even conduct a three-dimensional tour of what they had drawn. My blindness prompted the customer to get even more involved than if a sighted salesperson had done the same presentation.

After a few years we decided to close the doors, and I started doing sales again, working for several different companies that manufactured specialized disk systems and tape backup systems for customers who processed large amounts of business-critical data and needed a safe and secure method to store their records. We helped sell systems that could create and maintain data libraries for businesses in the areas of health care, government, education, media and entertainment, and finance.

I loved my job and did my selling both by phone and in person. When I set up appointments, I usually didn't tell people I was blind, not because I thought it would make a difference but because I just didn't think to tell them. But the longer I worked in sales, the more I began to realize my blindness had a certain value in selling. I don't mean I tried to make people feel sorry for me. I don't think I ever made a sale that was motivated by the customer's pity for me, feeling sorry for the blind guy. That's one card I never play because I don't see it as a handicap in the first place.

But one area where my blindness came in handy was in product demonstrations. When I was on a sales call and I set up the product and took the customer through the steps of operating and troubleshooting the products, I could almost hear the wheels turning in the customers' heads. "Gee . . . if a blind man can operate this, then anybody can."

Then there was the dog factor. Having a guide dog proved to be helpful in certain situations. Customers were more open to having conversations, and even if I could sense they were giving me dirty looks, they might not shoo me out the door as quickly. I worked hard to build relationships, to determine what the customer needed, and to solve problems with creative solutions. If I didn't have a workable solution, I suggested alternatives. After I did everything I could do, I would stop talking, ask for the order, and wait. And I did well.

As I worked my way up from humble sales rep to sales manager, I traveled hundreds of thousands of miles, and I worked with some great people at a company called Artecon.

My sales reps and I had a good time. I used to egg them on to make their sales calls by telling them we were "dialing for dollars," a theme I took from a low-budget TV game show by the same name. We worked in cubicles and I kept the atmosphere fun and lighthearted.

Once a month I rounded up all the salespeople, and we piled into a motor home and headed to George's Burgers, a greasy joint in San Marcos. One time they let me drive the motor home in the parking lot. "Just put the thing in D for Drive," they told me.

"When I hit the bumps, the Braille keeps me in between the lines," I said.

One of my favorite sales reps of all time was Billie Castillo. She was a firecracker and didn't know much about technology when she started, but she made up for it in moxie and energy. "I was a sales rookie who didn't know the difference between computer disk and tape, and you turned me into the World Wide Web Queen," she said recently.

Billie didn't much like to fly, especially in the winter when they were de-icing the wings of airplanes. She always said I had a calming effect on her. "Something about your personality, your no-fear thing. You're so used to adapting and reacting to the environment."

I traveled a lot of miles with Billie. We developed a great strategy using my guide dog Klondike at trade shows when we took walks around the other booths to check out our competitors' products. Klondike would draw attention with people wanting to touch him or ask questions. "Oh, your dog is so cute. Can I pet him?"

After we gathered a group of dog lovers, we'd slowly saunter back to our booth with

Klondike, bringing the crowd with us. Once or twice Klondike accidentally stepped on power cords and interrupted the power supply to other booths. But who could get angry at a beautiful golden retriever?

In 1996, I ended up with an office in the World Trade Center for the first time when I opened up a regional sales office in New York City for Artecon.

One thing that impressed me about the World Trade Center was the stringent security. After the bombings in '93, they put strict measures in place to control and monitor who went in and out of the buildings. In the lobby, you were asked to provide your ID. If you were a visitor, they either checked your name off of a clearance list or called up the company you were headed to in order to verify that you were expected. After your identity was verified and your visit authorized, they took a photo and created a badge for you with a bar code. But just because you had a badge didn't mean you had the run of the building; the badge limited your access to certain floors only.

A few years and a couple of jobs later, I ended up in the World Trade Center again, this time with Quantum. In the year 2000 we opened an office on the 78th floor of Tower 1, the North Tower. I was regional sales manager, and this time I got an all-access security badge from the Port Authority, which meant I could go anywhere in the building, including the underground parking garages. I kept up my habit of taking a different route each time, and I explored the building and developed an array of shortcuts. Before I ever brought my guide dog, I used my white cane and explored the building, constructing my mental map so I would always know where I was.

One of my best sales reps ever was Kevin Washington. If you can sell in New York, you can sell anywhere. And Kevin could sell in New York. He was a hoot and always gave me a hard time. He started calling my white cane a "ninja stick." He also liked to challenge me and try to get me lost. He would walk with me to a certain point in a basement or parking garage then walk away and see if I could find him. He was fascinated with how I navigated, so he called me Batman "because you have built-in radar like a bat."

"We all know you can see," Kevin used to joke. "Come on . . . there's no way you can't see."

Once, Kevin and I were walking down the street together with my guide dog. The sidewalk was crowded, and a woman coming the opposite direction neglected to move aside, bumped into me, and fell down. We helped her up, and she came up fighting mad. She shouted at Kevin, "You're his handler. You should be more careful."

Kevin and I both reacted when we realized she wasn't talking about the dog, she was talking about Kevin. Handler? If ever I was tempted to use my white cane as a ninja stick, that would have been the time. But Kevin and I just laughed it off.

A feisty and opinionated New Yorker, Kevin was a huge help in dealing with the New York cabdrivers. Many of them were uncomfortable with dogs in their cabs, and if I stood on the curb, they'd pass me by. It wasn't easy for me to catch a cab. So Kevin would stand at the curb and hail a cab while I stayed back out of sight. When the taxi stopped, I'd run forward with Roselle and join him. If the driver still balked, Kevin would unleash his New York City bluster. "Look, this is a working dog. You pull away and we'll report you to the Taxi License Commission. And I have friends in Homeland Security. Don't mess with us." We did file a few complaints to the NYC Taxi and Limo Commission against cabdrivers who refused to transport us. We probably helped finance the city budget with those complaints.

On September 11, Kevin happened to oversleep because he'd been up late the night before playing with his beautiful one-year-old baby girl. He ended up going into work late and was on the PATH train, just entering the tube under the Hudson River, when the first plane hit our tower. The ground vibrated, and the train stopped then reversed and went back to Jersey City. With the trains stopped, he was stuck in Jersey City. He watched the towers fall, not knowing whether his Quantum colleagues were dead or alive. I had expected Kevin that morning, as he had a 10 a.m. appointment with people from Cantor Fitzgerald on the 102nd floor of Tower 1. He had not arrived by the time we left, but I didn't know until later what had happened to him.

When David, Roselle, and I hit the concourse, the shopping mall under the World Trade Center, we begin to run. More water. We still don't know exactly what is going on, but from the commotion in the lobby, it's pretty clear that we need to get out and away. The shops in the mall are deserted, and the human traffic is flowing the same direction: up and out. We take an escalator and ride it up and outside to the second-floor plaza.

For the first time since the chaos began, we step into New York sunlight. We stop and breathe in some fresh air. It seems like a lifetime since we heard the explosion. I check my watch. It's been an hour, almost to the minute.

David looks around, then up at the towers. "There's a fire in Tower 2, up high," he says.

What? The explosion was in Tower 1. What is going on?

We're confused. What is happening? *Maybe when our building tipped, the fire jumped to the other tower.* We can't think of any other explanation. The stairwell had been like an isolation chamber, blocking us from any outside news.

But we're about to find out.

9
RUNNING WITH ROSELLE

Faith is taking the first step even when
you don't see the whole staircase.
                    MARTIN LUTHER KING JR.

Waves of people approach. First, the paramedics. "Thank you, but we're fine. No injuries here."

Next come the television reporters, asking for comments, but we are still in flight mode, and we keep moving. People fill the streets, streaming in all directions.

We pause for a moment on the southwest corner of Broadway and Ann, about a hundred yards away from Tower 2, the South Tower. David takes out his camera to take a picture of the gray and black smoke billowing upward from the towers while I try to reach Karen on my cell phone to let her know we are safe. All I can get, though, is an "All circuits are busy" message. We learned later that that the overloading of the cellular phone system was due to the many trapped people on the upper floors calling loved ones to say good-bye.

We still don't know exactly what happened to cause the explosion and the fires. We won't find out until later that the blaze in the towers is so intense it is reaching temperatures as high as 2,000 degrees and generating heat equivalent to three to five times the energy output of a nuclear power plant.[1] Fireproofing, sprinkler systems, and the water supply for fire hoses have been knocked out, although the fire is so extensive that sprinklers might not be much help anyway. The plane's impact between the 78th and 84th floors destroyed exterior columns and may have also damaged interior columns and the floor plate. The floors near the impact suffered severe damage. But the fire is the key problem, heating up the structure to a critical point. Molten aluminum from the plane is flowing down the side of the building opposite the initial impact.

It's 9:59 a.m., just over an hour since we left our offices. David puts away his camera, and I am closing up my cell phone, unable to reach Karen, when a police officer screams, "Get out of here! It's coming down!"

The South Tower emits a deep rumble that becomes a deafening roar. I hear glass breaking and metal tearing, accompanied by a chorus of shrill and terrified screams. I will never forget that sound as long as I live. It was like a cross between a freight train and a waterfall of breaking glass.

A floor up in the southeast corner started the ball rolling with a partial collapse, along with columns along the east face buckling near the floor from south to north. Then the top of the building twisted to the east and south, crashing downward and taking successive floors out like dominoes. The South Tower was down in just ten seconds in a cacophonous waterfall of glass, steel, and people.

The impact creates a vibration that travels through my feet and up my legs, and the street feels like a trampoline bouncing. A jolt of fear rips through me and my throat freezes; I can't even scream.

David cries, "Oh, my God!" and starts running. In a split second's time I swing 180 degrees, lifting Roselle up bodily and spinning around with a death grip on her harness, and we break into a run too. We are running for our lives. No one is helping anyone anymore.

Except for Roselle and me. We are still

there for each other.

Rocks, metal, and glass fall around us, and small hard objects pelt my head and face.

For the second time today, I think that I might die, this time without even being able to say good-bye to Karen.

Many people did perish in the streets surrounding the towers, crushed by the falling building, flattened by debris, or blasted by the shock wave. There were eyewitness reports of eight-ton steel I-beams tumbling end over end. Cars launched through the air along with chunks of concrete, metal ductwork, and shards of glass. One report tells of an EMT firefighter who survived while a flying I-beam killed his partner right next to him.

Roselle and I run away from the noise. I don't understand why this is happening. My heart cries out to God in anguish.

How could you get us out of the building only to have it fall on us?

As soon as I silently scream out the question, God answers. I hear his voice inside my head and my heart. He speaks directly to me.

Don't worry about what you cannot control. Focus on running with Roselle, and the rest will take care of itself.

I'd never before heard God's voice so

close and so clearly. Immediately I feel peace and a sense of protection. My mind and my heart begin to settle down, and I start to focus on Roselle. The harness feels solid in my hand, and our bond is sure.

But now I am stronger and more confident. I know beyond any shadow of a doubt that God is directing me just as I direct Roselle.

The noise becomes more intense, debris showering the streets. We reach Fulton Street, which we had crossed only a few moments before. After turning right on Fulton, David and I somehow find each other, and we stop for a moment, all of us panting from the adrenaline-powered flight. It turns out he had run in the same direction.

Then comes the cloud.

A monstrous dust cloud three hundred feet high roars at us, enveloping us in a thick, toxic blanket of smoke, gases, vapors, and pulverized concrete dust. The cloud moves too fast and we cannot get away. We're blasted with sand and gravel.

My body tenses up but there is nothing else to do but inhale. The dust and debris fill my throat and my lungs. I am drowning, trying to breathe through dirt. The dust is so thick I can feel it going down my throat every time I take a breath. I feel like I'm dying, the dust filling up my body and choking the life out of me.

Somehow I hang on to Roselle's harness and we keep moving. Roselle is right alongside, guiding perfectly. She never stops.

Guide dogs are specially bred and trained to focus. When they are first received from the puppy raisers and brought back to the Guide Dogs for the Blind school for training with a certified guide dog instructor, each dog is given a temperament assessment during which the instructors note the dog's reaction to different situations such as run-ins with other dogs and cats, exposure to food, noise, and other circumstances likely to produce anxiety in the average dog. Fifty percent of the puppies wash out. Dogs who maintain concentration and focus move forward in the training; they have the potential to do well in the intensive months-long course of guide dog training.

Roselle passed that test back when she was a puppy, demonstrating the intelligence and steadfastness I need now. Enveloped in the cloud, she continues to work and to guide even though her eyes, nose, and mouth are full of dust and debris too. Roselle's guide dog training could never have prepared her for anything like this, but she is brave and she does not quit; instead, she uses whatever senses she can muster to watch out for me.

Whatever happens, whether we live or whether we die, we are in this together. If we don't make it out alive, I hope we stay together, my hand on Roselle's harness. I will never let go.

In tough times one of my favorite biblical passages is Psalm 23, and the older I get, the more I realize that life isn't just about green pastures and still water. Just like in the psalm, life also includes hot, dusty roads; deserts; enemies; and sometimes, fire.

Psalm 23

The LORD is my shepherd; I shall not want. He makes me to lie down in green pastures; He leads me beside the still waters.

He restores my soul; He leads me in the paths of righteousness for His name's sake.

Yea, though I walk through the valley of the shadow of death, I will fear no evil;

For You are with me; Your rod and Your staff, they comfort me.

You prepare a table before me in the presence of my enemies; You anoint my head with oil; my cup runs over.

Surely goodness and mercy shall follow me

All the days of my life;

And I will dwell in the house of the LORD forever.

My dad taught me to love God. Not only did we spend a lot of time over the years working together on electronics, math, scouting, and doing ham radio but we also talked about bigger things like: Who created the universe? Why are we here? Who is in control? What is the purpose of life? I could bring just about any question to my dad and he was willing to talk to me about it. In a lot of ways, we were kindred spirits.

My father did a lot of reading on Christianity, and he read to me often. When I was in fourth grade, I came home from school one day to find several big boxes waiting for me. Inside was a Braille Bible, King James Version, in eighteen large volumes. It takes up almost five feet of shelf space and still occupies prime real estate in my home office.

My mother was Jewish, and her ideas about religion tended to be wrapped up in Jewish holidays and challah and chicken soup with delicious matzo balls. She never attended synagogue, but she did go to church with us at St. Stephen's Lutheran Church in Palmdale. I sang tenor in the choir and we attended services every Sunday, although I sometimes found the sermons boring. Rather than sitting and listening to the preacher, I liked exploring the

Bible on my own and having discussions with my dad. Our talks ranged all over the place, and we talked about different faiths and ways that people worshipped God. But for me, faith always comes back to a friendship with God.

"There is not in the world a kind of life more sweet and delightful than that of a continual conversation with God," said Brother Lawrence. A lay brother in a Carmelite monastery in Paris, Brother Lawrence wrote *The Practice of the Presence of God* about maintaining a profound awareness of God moment by moment, no matter the situation.

On the ground in desperate flight from the collapsing tower is not the first time I prayed on September 11. I started praying up in the tower after the first explosion, listening for anything God had to say. Just as listening is the most important part of successful selling, it is also the most important part of prayer. It's how I try to live my life, constantly asking, *Am I doing the right thing? Is this what I'm supposed to do? Is this the right path to take?*

Looking to God for direction is where Psalm 23 starts. Its first words are a simple statement of trust in God with "The LORD is my shepherd." In fact, the whole psalm is one of trust, a vow to put oneself in the hands of the living God.

The psalm's author, David, had been a shepherd in his youth, just like my father, so the psalm is very special to me. But the shepherd-and-sheep image also reminds me of the relationship between my guide dog and me. Everything hinges on Roselle's initial acceptance of me as her leader. While she helps me in very important ways by keeping me out of holes and making sure I don't walk in front of a speeding electric car (which doesn't make much noise), it is ultimately my job to plan out our route and to direct her. If she doesn't trust me as her shepherd and respond to my tugs on her harness or my verbal commands, our relationship can't work.

Because Roselle and I are a team, I take care of her. I provide for her wants with food and water, usually in the evenings, in order to minimize her need to relieve herself during the day, especially during long days of air or train travel. She isn't allowed to eat from the table at home or in restaurants. This is a constant temptation for her because many people would like to feed her, and I often have to turn down succulent bits of steak and chicken from well-meaning restaurant owners and servers.

Roselle's fear of thunderstorms reminds me of my dad telling me about how fearful sheep are, afraid of anything new or unexpected. Sheep can't sleep and won't eat unless they feel safe and secure. They're also afraid of fast-moving water, so it's up to the shepherd to find quiet, comfortable places, green pastures, and still waters where the sheep can sleep, eat, and drink. During thunderstorms, Roselle's safe haven was under my desk in the basement at home, her head on my feet. When the South Tower suddenly gave way and we were overtaken by the airborne dust and debris, we needed a sanctuary too.

Because Roselle trusts me and because we've worked together enough to become a team and to know each other's habits, she listens to my voice. When I correct her, she stops and listens, trying to figure out what I want her to do. It's the same with the shepherd. As the relationship grows, the sheep learn to follow his voice "in the paths of righteousness." Then, when difficult times come and the sheep have to walk through dangerous situations, God is there, guiding.

When he worked as a shepherd, my dad used a rod and staff to guide and protect the sheep. I have my white cane and the guide dog harness instead. God uses more sophisticated and even mysterious ways to guide and protect, but even though I don't always understand how he works, I am comforted and confident knowing that he is at work in my life.

When the day ends and Roselle's harness comes off, she can rest. She knows she's part of the family, and she has her own bed, her own dog toys and chew bone, and her own food and water bowl. When work is over, she can play, eat, and relax. She is an important part of our family, just as I'm an important part of God's family and an honored guest at God's table. Even when there are enemies about, I can eat and drink of God's goodness in safety at his side. I am special to him.

I've had many other dogs, but there is only one Roselle. And I know her. I know the feel of her ears and her neck, the nudge of her nose against my hand, and the lean of her powerful body against my calf. I know the sound of her happy bark, her drowsy snore, and her sad little whine. She was specially trained and set apart for me by Guide Dogs for the Blind, and she is unique. There is no other guide dog, or any dog, exactly like her.

And God knows me. He made me. He has

studied me and watched over me, and he loves me. He "anoints my head with oil." In the Middle East, hosts used to anoint their honored guests at banquets with oil on their hair and beards; it was meant to invigorate and refresh. Anointing also could be used to set someone aside as holy or sacred, meant for a special purpose. Part of the fun and challenge of living has been discovering my purpose. What was I designed for? How can I use what I have learned and the experiences I've been through to help others? Roselle knows her purpose. I am still discovering and living out mine.

God's goodness and mercy follow me every day, like the shepherd follows after his sheep. He pursues each one until he brings it safely home, as in the story told by Jesus of the shepherd who left his flock of ninety-nine to find one lost sheep, rejoicing when he found and rescued it.

I heard a story about a man visiting Yellowstone National Park with his dog. They were hiking among the mineral springs, some of which contain water superheated by geothermal forces above the boiling point to temperatures of two hundred degrees Fahrenheit and above. He unleashed his dog, which promptly ran off and jumped into one of the springs. The dog yelped and began to struggle as the water seared his flesh. His owner hesitated for a moment then jumped in after his dog. There is no happy ending to this story; both perished. But I have always remembered the man's extravagant love for his dog and his decision to chance death in the boiling water.

When the tower fell and I cried out to God, his answer gave me hope. When God is for us, who can be against us? There is hope for the future. I am part of God's family, and "I will dwell in the house of the LORD forever."

I didn't tell anyone about my encounter with God that day under the shadow of the tower. I didn't tell anyone the next day or even the next week. It was such a powerful moment, so intimate and so personal, that I didn't share it with anyone for three or four years. I wanted to be able to present it right, and I didn't want it to be some hokey, manipulative thing. I didn't want to wear my miracle on my sleeve. I prayed about what to do, and slowly, as time passed, I grew more comfortable talking about my life-and-death moment, my desperate cry, and God's response, and it slowly became a public part of my story. Some people might not believe it or might judge it wishful thinking or something that came out of my own heart and mind. Some people might even get angry, knowing that God didn't answer the same prayers offered up by others. But he did answer mine.

I found out later that other people were praying for me that day besides Karen. A dear friend of ours, the Reverend K. Cherie Jones, was pastor of Atascadero United Methodist Church in California's Central Coast. We met her when she was pastoring a church in San Marcos, California, close to where we lived. We three hit it off and began a lifelong friendship, growing very close when a good friend of Cherie's was brutally murdered by her ex-husband. Her friend's body was discovered six months later, and it was two and a half years before the murderer was sent to prison. Karen and I stayed in close contact with Cherie during that difficult time, exchanging countless e-mails, phone calls, and prayers as she grieved.

On September 11, Cherie happened to wake up at 6:15 a.m. and flipped on the TV, as usual, to check the local news and weather. But something strange was going on. Instead of the familiar faces of the morning news anchors, Katie Couric and the Today Show people were on, along with startling images of New York City on fire. It

173

had been about thirty minutes since the first explosion and just fifteen minutes since the second. Cherie was confused. *The* Today *show isn't supposed to be on,* she thought. Then she thought of two people: me, wondering if I still worked in the WTC, and a parishioner who was a pilot for Delta Airlines with a regular West to East Coast route.

Cherie began to pray for both of us, for the emergency responders, and for the other people in the towers. She called the pilot's wife and found out he was on the ground, safe. Next she tried Karen to see if I was okay but couldn't get through.

Then she got down to business. Cherie started calling her prayer warriors to work the church directories. "You take pages 1 and 2; call everybody and tell them to pray and then meet us at the church at 9 a.m.," she told the first one. She kept calling, dividing up the work of contacting the congregation, then headed over to the church. Forty people ended up joining her, and they began to pray for us, for the people in the towers and the Pentagon, for those still in the air, and for the city and the nation. The United States was under attack, and no one knew what was going to happen next. But God certainly knew, and he was hearing a lot about it from the people of Atascadero.

When Cherie first started praying for us, David, Roselle, and I were in the stairwell on about the 10th floor. When she started calling people, we were out on the street, fleeing the towers. When the South Tower collapsed, she saw it on TV and began praying for me in earnest, not knowing if I was still inside or not. I may just owe my life to my wife, my family, my friends, and a woman out on the West Coast in her pajamas, praying for me by name as Roselle and I walked through the valley of the shadow of death.

Sometimes walking, sometimes running, we stay on the sidewalk and move west on Fulton Street, searching for a refuge. I can barely breathe, but I can still hear, and I listen for an opening. I keep telling Roselle, "Right . . . right," hoping she will find an open doorway. She listens, and through the harness I can tell she is looking. I don't know if she can see anything, but I'm trusting she will use her nose and her ears to find an opening for us.

We have to get out of the dust or we are going to die. But even in the dust cloud, with my guide dog now blind, too, I feel

God's presence. He is with me. I am not alone. I am running with Roselle.

10
WE ARE PRETTY MUCH JUST LIKE YOU

This is the true joy in life — being used
for a purpose recognized by yourself as a
mighty one; being thoroughly worn out
before you are thrown on the scrap heap;
being a force of nature instead of a
feverish selfish little clod of ailments and
grievances complaining that the world will
not devote itself to making you happy.

GEORGE BERNARD SHAW

Debris showers the streets. The horrific sounds continue as the South Tower rubble settles, concrete, steel, and glass groaning and grinding its way downward.

We are running along the sidewalk when Roselle and I hear an opening. "Right," I cry out. I feel an overwhelming yearning to be inside a safe and secure building that isn't going to collapse or burst into flames.

David goes with us. Just after Roselle turns and goes into the opening, she stops, the first time she's stopped all day without my direction. *What does she see? She wouldn't stop without good reason.*

I slide my right foot out and feel the edge of a step and I can hear the echo of a stairwell going down. Roselle has stopped me at the top of a long flight of stairs. I still don't feel safe, though. I want to get farther away from the hellish situation outside. I need a safe place to breathe and regroup. So does Roselle. I'm not sure where we are yet, but I trust her, and we are going in.

We've already navigated down 1,463 stairs today. What are a few more?

"Forward," I say. We rush in, leaving the death and destruction and chaos behind. At least for a while.

David wipes at his eyes and tries to make out the sign: FULTON STREET SUBWAY STATION. As we walk down the stairs, we're rubbing our eyes and wiping our noses and brushing off the dust as best we can. I'm coughing and snorting, trying to clear my lungs.

Roselle is panting; then she sneezes a few times. *I wonder how she's doing. Going through something like this must be pushing her to exhaustion.* But she doesn't show any strain. Her walk is light, steady, and sure. The noise of the tower settling, along with

178

the emergency vehicles and frenzied voices outside, must be alarming to her sharp canine ears. But she gives no sign that it bothers her.

We reach the bottom of the stairs and discover a larger space. It turns out to be a small arcade leading into the subway station. I hear crying.

"I can't see! My eyes are full of dirt," a woman wails. "I can't see! I don't want to fall into the subway."

I give Roselle a nudge with the harness, and we walk toward the voice. I'm no superhero, but I think I can help.

I reach out with my right hand and touch her arm.

She quiets.

I gently take her arm and tuck it into mine.

"Please don't worry." I keep my voice measured and low. "I am blind, and I have a guide dog named Roselle. She will help us and keep us from falling down the stairs into the subway." Roselle stands quietly, waiting.

The woman responds, clutching my arm. This time the blind really is leading the blind, but why should that be unusual? After all, helping this lady is what teamwork is all about.

I hear someone coming up the stairs from

farther down in the station. It's a man, he says his name is Lou, and he works in the subway. "Follow me," he says, his voice urgent.

Other refugees have wandered in from the street, and now there are eight of us. Lou leads the group down the stairs and a hallway and then through a doorway into the employee locker room. It's quiet inside, clean and cool. An oscillating fan stirs the air. There is a water fountain against the wall, and we take turns cleaning up and washing out our eyes and mouths. Water never tasted so good. Roselle flops down to rest on the cool floor.

When not at the water fountain, we sit on the locker room benches and rest. My head is spinning. So much has happened in such a short time, and my mind reels, going over the events and trying to make sense of the explosion, the fire, the freight train/waterfall noise, and the dust cloud. But even though my mind is racing, trying to put the pieces together in some sort of order, my heart is calm and peaceful. I relive the sound of the building's collapse and my desperate prayer. *God's voice was so clear. And I still feel that same inner peace, even though we almost died.*

I know others have died. There could be

hundreds or even thousands who have perished in the fire, the building collapse, or from the debris. I could have so easily died if the building had fallen a little differently, if we had taken a different path, or if we had moved at a slower pace.

What if we had worked for a while longer trying to shut down the computers in the office before we left? We could still be in the stairwell right now. But we are not. Roselle and I are here, safe for the moment, underground with a guy named Lou.

God spared my life and he spoke to me. There must be a reason. But I don't have time to figure it out because just then, a police officer bursts into the locker room. He is covered in dust too.

"The air is starting to clear," he says. "It's time to move out. I have orders to evacuate the station." I check my watch. We've been in the station about ten minutes, but we follow his orders. Who knows what else is going to happen? I'm anxious to get out and farther away from this whole area. I want to know what is going on, and I want to try to call Karen again. She must be frantic.

Instantly Roselle stands up with me, ready to work. As a group, we follow the police officer, walking quietly.

What will we find outside?

Once, Karen and I were visiting her brother, who lived in the mountains of Idaho. It was a beautiful day, and we decided to take a walk. His nine-year-old daughter asked me a surprising question: "How can you go take a walk?" Of course she meant no offense, but her question put into words a common misconception: that somehow blindness equates to a lack of ability, or even to incompetence. Even though she had spent considerable time with me while we lived in New Jersey, she still couldn't conceive of how a blind person could walk independently.

If there is just one message about blindness that I could share with sighted people, it would be this: It's okay to be blind. It won't ruin your life or drain away all joy and satisfaction. It won't strangle your creativity or lower your intelligence. It won't keep you from traveling and experiencing life in other places. It won't separate you from friends and family. It won't keep you from falling in love, getting married, and having a family of your own. It won't prevent you from getting a job and making a living. Blindness doesn't mean the end of the world. And with technology and education, blindness can be reduced from an all-consuming disability to just another human limitation, of which there are many. There is more to life than eye function.

The legal definition of blindness is visual acuity of less than 20/200 with correction or a field of less than 20 degrees; there are people all over the spectrum in regard to sight. Some people can see light but cannot discern objects. Some people have fuzzy vision but can still navigate and walk down the sidewalk without help. Some people see nothing. So how do you define blindness? The human definition of blindness, according to Kenneth Jernigan, a civil rights pioneer for the blind and past president of the National Federation of the Blind, is a little different from the legal definition: "A person is blind to the extent that the individual must devise alternative techniques to do efficiently those things which he or she would do if they had normal vision."[1] So blind people are still able-bodied, with full command of their intelligence and abilities; they just use alternative techniques on their journey through life. And sometimes those techniques can even be superior to the techniques of light-dependent people.

Laura Sloate is a managing director for a

Wall Street investment management firm. She has been blind since the age of six. In an interview with the *New York Times,* she talked about how she reads constantly for her job, spending hours keeping up with the news from the *Wall Street Journal* and other industry news sources. She uses her computer's text-to-speech system to play the *Economist* (magazine) aloud at the pace of three hundred words a minute. At the same time, an assistant reads the *Financial Times* to her, and "she devotes one ear to the paper and the other to the magazine."[2]

If you happen to call me on the telephone, while we are talking, I may also be catching up on e-mail or reading documents at the same time. So during our conversation, you just might hear a low-pitched, digitized man's voice muttering in the background. Once you get the hang of it, it's not that difficult to keep up with a screen reader at high speeds, and it's not uncommon for blind people to listen to screen readers at three hundred, four hundred, or even five hundred words a minute.

Blindness doesn't mean inferiority. When Kenneth Jernigan took over the presidency of the National Federation of the Blind, he began his leadership of a movement based on the belief that "a blind person can compete at almost anything on terms of equality with a sighted person."[3]

Currently, there are successful blind architects, engineers, attorneys, doctors, teachers, scientists, mathematicians, businesspeople, musicians, and artists. A war veteran named Scott Smiley, who lost his sight to a massive car bomb in the northern part of Iraq, is the Army's first blind active-duty officer. He also competes in triathlons, skis, and jumps out of planes. He has summited Mount Rainier and surfed solo in Hawaii.[4] Erik Weihenmayer is a mountain climber who became the first blind man in history to reach the summit of Mount Everest. He has also conquered the Seven Summits, climbing the highest peak on every continent. David Blunkett is a member of Parliament in Britain. Blind since birth and raised in a very poor family, he served as Tony Blair's education secretary then served as home secretary from 2001 to 2004. A blind photographer named Pete Eckert recently won a major photography competition in New York City. His work was singled out over hundreds of submissions from photographers in fourteen countries. "I am not bound by the assumptions of the sighted or their assumed limits," he said in a recent interview. "The camera is another means of making art to me."[5]

In a recent conversation, Marc Maurer, the current president of National Federation of the Blind, was asked for a list of professions that are still largely off-limits to blind people. He came up with two. Professional sports are very visually oriented, and while blind people participate in athletics all the time, to be a competitive football player with the technology available is "quite unlikely." The second area off-limits to the blind is any job that requires professional driving. "Beyond those two, I haven't identified any others," said Dr. Maurer.

While pro football might be off-limits for a while, driving blind could just be in my very near future. While I've driven a car a few times around Palmdale, UC Irvine, and the parking lot at George's Burgers with my sales force, it was always brief and just for fun. I needed a sighted person as a guide because the technology did not exist for me to drive public roads safely and legally. But that is changing, with some new technology in development under Dr. Dennis Hong, a professor of mechanical engineering and director of the Robotics and Mechanisms Laboratory at Virginia Tech. The project is designed to allow blind people to independently drive automobiles one day through novel nonvisual user interfaces. I haven't had the chance to try it out yet since it's still in development, but I've heard it involves a special steering wheel used to communicate with and direct the car. A second-generation prototype is now in the works, using a modified 2010 Ford Hybrid Escape with even better interface technology. Someday soon I'll be able to take Karen out for a drive.

The technology revolution that began with Ray Kurzweil and his reading machine for the blind is still rolling, with the need for technology in the blind community driving innovation in the larger business community. The success of the reading machine also demonstrated that "addressing the problem of blindness by building a piece of technology that is useful for blind people means there quite often will be additional technological developments resulting from that piece of technology that would be useful and sellable to the rest of society," said Dr. Maurer. The needs of blind people are driving technological advances for all drivers. Besides the smart driver technology that, when adopted by the big automobile manufacturers, will help make driving safer for everyone, blind technology has been adopted and developed for many other uses.

There are some extraordinary GPS devices in development that will make it to the sighted market at some point. Kurzweil developed dictation technology that has crossed over and is built into the Dragon NaturallySpeaking computer programs. And a new e-book reader called Blio will be released by the time this book appears. Blio is a platform-independent piece of software first developed for the blind, but now available for all to read books and magazines on a computer, phone, or other mobile device. The Blio will read books out loud, using lifelike, natural voices dubbed "Samantha" and "Tom," and will provide full-color pages in brilliant 3-D for the sighted.

Helping to drive these advances is National Federation of the Blind (NFB), the oldest and largest national organization led by blind people for blind people. There are fifty thousand members across the country, and most of them are not mountain climbers or army platoon leaders, just regular folks. "We who are blind are pretty much like you (a sighted person)," said Dr. Maurer. "We have our share of both geniuses and jerks but most of us are somewhere between, ordinary people leading ordinary lives." The NFB works hard to help ordinary blind people. Right now there are an estimated 1.8 million blind people in the U.S., "blind" meaning they have 10 percent or less of vision remaining and can no longer effectively operate as a sighted person. But with its fifty thousand members, NFB is making a significant impact on the blind population with its message of empowerment, a strong sense of community, and the education, tools, and resources offered to the blind by the blind. It is by far the largest organization of blind persons in the country and is the strongest representative of the blind in the nation.

The NFB serves as a watchdog organization. For example, the federation recently filed complaints with the government against Amazon, the mammoth online bookseller, to urge them to make the Amazon Kindle e-reader accessible to blind readers. The Kindle does have a primitive text-to-speech interface, but there is no method for people to get at the menus and operate the e-reader nonvisually. When the Kindle DX was marketed to colleges and universities for students to use in place of printed textbooks, Dr. Maurer said he remembers thinking, *Wait just a second, now. You're creating a barrier to reading. Blind people have as much right to read as anyone else. Reading is a fundamental right — it has*

*to be — otherwise you're creating two groups:
one that is literate and one that is not.*

The NFB is also working with the federal government to provide raised markers on paper money so blind people can distinguish one denomination from another. (I get around this by putting special folds on my cash bills, a different one for each denomination, so I can tell the difference. An unscrupulous person could still try to cheat me when making change. But my trusty K-NFB Reader has a special currency mode and can read bills.) The NFB has also been lobbying car manufacturers to add sound to electric cars, which are almost silent. Think about it: if you are blind and walking through a parking lot, an electric car with a virtually silent engine could easily make short work of you if its driver didn't happen to spot you first. This effort is meeting with some success. Recently Nissan added a soft whine to the Nissan Leaf's engine. The noise fluctuates in intensity with the car's speed and makes a clanging sound in reverse.

Other car manufacturers are working on similar projects. Congress just passed a bill signed into law by the president on January 3, 2011, to require the government to research methodologies for quiet vehicles to provide audible sounds for the safety of all pedestrians and to create rules which will require manufacturers to incorporate appropriate audible signals in all quiet cars. This law came about because of the imagination and active participation of the 50,000 members of the National Federation of the Blind.

I grew up in the sighted community, mainstreamed by my parents. For the most part I never got the chance to be around other blind people and had no sense of the larger blind community. I thought I was doing pretty darn well on my own with my guide dog Squire. And because I did well in school, I began to develop a bit of an attitude, especially toward blind people who struggled more to cope with the challenges. In reality, I didn't even know how to use a cane yet, and I was locked in my own little academic world, unaware that there were other blind people out there who might have something to offer me, and me to them.

That all changed when I got involved with the NFB. I first became aware of the organization when I won a scholarship my senior year of high school and went to the NFB state convention in California to pick it up. Kenneth Jernigan spoke. I listened, opening up to the possibility that I could learn something from this group of people. Jernigan was an engaging, charismatic speaker who had that magical quality of being able to energize and inspire people to new ways of thinking. He was fearless and he was brilliant. His talk was an elegant argument against the status quo and a clarion call for change. (You can read the text of one of his best-known talks at the back of this book.) Jernigan wanted nothing more than a revolution, a civil rights movement for the blind. I left with my head spinning. His voice rang in my ears: "The real problem is not the blindness but the mistaken attitudes about it. These attitudes can be changed, and we are changing them."[6]

Later that year, I went to a six-week college prep course by the California State Department of Rehabilitation for incoming blind college freshman. It was my first exposure to living in a community of blind people and my first time using a cane. I didn't want to seem ignorant, though, and bought a cane from the Braille Institute a few days before so I could try it out and do some practice. I quickly got the hang of it. One night my mobility instructor issued a challenge: after dinner, we would see who could make it back to the dorm first, him or me. He would wear a secure blindfold.

Game on.

The instructor and I worked our way back neck and neck until we hit a large parking lot with a lot of ins and outs. I found my way pretty quickly, drawing on my hard-earned echolocation skills. My poor instructor got lost, poking around the parking lot with his white cane for almost two hours. As you might imagine, this little exercise did nothing to throttle down my ego.

In college I was busy with academics and my radio show, but my senior year, a guy named Don Brown, president of the Orange County chapter of the NFB, called me up and talked me into joining. A couple of years later, I was nominated for president of the chapter. But I started to feel like an outsider, and it seemed as if people were a little standoffish. I called organization leader Gary Mackenstadt. He told me the truth.

"Michael, you're arrogant. People here have a lot more experience than you, and it's up to you to get to know them." I felt as though I'd walked straight into a telephone pole.

"You are not the only blind person out there. There are a lot of other blind people who have worked together and shared experiences. It can't always be your way. You have to meet people in the middle."

Gary cared enough about me to share the truth in love, and it was a much needed wake-up call. He became a mentor to me, and I realized there was a big world out there in terms of the blind community. But in order to join it and be a contributing member, I needed to offer myself for service, not act like a know-it-all who was there to set people straight. I realized that every time one blind person takes a step forward, so does the whole community.

After that much-needed attitude adjustment, my involvement with NFB grew, and when I eventually found myself working for them on the Kurzweil Reader, I got the opportunity to meet the movers and shakers in the organization. I hit it off with Dr. Maurer. We had a lot in common: he had also been blinded as a newborn from excess oxygen, we both loved science, and we were both pretty opinionated. I participated in a number of demonstrations and walks on the Capitol and interacted with national political leaders. And I always had fun. I guess that's the salesman in me. You've got to have fun.

In my early NFB days I spent some time with Hazel tenBroek, wife of NFB founder Jacobus "Chick" tenBroek. Dr. tenBroek founded the NFB in 1940 in Berkeley, where he was a professor and chair of the speech department. After his untimely death, I had the opportunity to spend a week at Mrs. tenBroek's house to help her with some filing and other tasks related to her job as editor of the *Braille Monitor*. I soaked in her hospitality, along with the history and legacy of this amazing couple who had led the charge for blind civil rights. Dr. tenBroek had advocated social welfare reforms based in constitutional law, and he helped lay the groundwork for the legal protections blind people enjoy today. My fondest memory from my time in Berkeley with Mrs. tenBroek was walking down the hill after dinner to Batz's Ice Cream Parlor, buying a quart of their gourmet ice cream, and having it for breakfast with her the next day.

The NFB has strengthened me, encouraged me, equipped me, and empowered me to live and to work with confidence and freedom. I've had the privilege of becoming a part of a community of blind people who are living abundant, joyful lives and the privilege of serving in a civil rights movement that will guarantee our blind children and grandchildren access to education, literacy, satisfying employment, and purposeful lives.

It's a big world and I'm excited to be a part of it and to serve people, blind or sighted, in any way I can. Oh, and don't forget to keep one eye on the rearview mirror. One of these days very soon, you might just see a blond-haired, light-eyed blind guy gaining on you in a snazzy, red sports car.

After being ejected from our subway station refuge, we climb the stairs and pass back through the door to the outside. There are no cars, but I hear people walking and running. No one is saying much. It's still smoky, but most of the cloud has passed, and the part that lingers is slowly settling onto the street, covering the debris in a thick layer of concrete dust. The sunlight feels great.

David speaks. His voice is full of shock and fear.

"There is no Tower 2," he says. All he sees is a pillar of smoke hundreds of feet high.

It's unthinkable. I can't wrap my mind around it even though I felt the vibration of the collapse and heard the noise.

I search for some other explanation. "Is it possible the smoke is hiding the tower?"

"No," says David. His voice is flat and toneless. "Mike, the tower is gone."

We stand there for a moment, David and

196

I. We clasp hands. Tower 2 has died, but we are alive. Two men and a dog.

We turn and walk west on Fulton Street, away from the World Trade Center. It's time to go home.

11
WOMAN ON WHEELS

Love makes your soul crawl out from its
hiding place.
ZORA NEALE HURSTON

It's 8:47 in the morning, and I'm watching
Good Morning America as I start to dress. As
usual, Mike was up bright and early and
left for work several hours ago. I heard him
leave, but it had been a rough night with
Roselle's panic attack, and I'm not a morning person anyway, so I drifted back to sleep
after he left.

For some reason, anchor Charlie Gibson's
face has just turned white. My phone rings.

With my eyes on the television, I reach for
the phone and hear Mike's voice. "Karen,
there's been an explosion of some sort.
We're okay, but we're leaving the building
now." His voice is quiet, but there's an edge
to it. After eighteen years of marriage, I can
tell when he's worried. I can also tell when

he is trying to stay calm.

"What happened?" I take a deep breath and wait for his answer. At the same time, I grab the TV remote off the nightstand.

"David, Roselle, and I are together. We're going to take the stairs." Click. I turn on the TV. No need to flip channels to see if the Twin Towers are in the news. They pop up immediately on the screen, gigantic plumes of jet-black smoke billowing from one of the towers.

"I'll call you again as soon as I can, but I have to go." I hear noise in the background, people talking, voices rushed.

"Okay, Mike. Be careful!" I want to add more, but he's already ended the call. There's so much more to say.

I watch. I can't believe what I'm seeing. It looks like ten or fifteen floors are engulfed in a horrific fire. *What happened? How could the fire have spread so fast?*

The television reporters seem confused and a little haphazard. No one is quite sure what is going on. Then the unthinkable happens. Out of nowhere there's a plane, moving fast, and it plows into the other building. The plane was huge, and it hit the side of the building and disappeared, as if the tower swallowed it up. A giant orange, gold, and black fireball erupts, pouring out of the tower. Debris that looks like silver match-sticks sprays out from the edges, but I know they are fragments of steel.

I can't believe what I'm seeing. It feels like I'm watching one of those melodramatic disaster movies. But this time it's real, and Mike is inside.

It's not long before the newspeople come up with video footage of the explosion in Mike's tower, and what they have been saying now becomes clear: his tower was hit by a huge commercial jet too. No one knows what is really going on, but the images are scaring me to death. The towers are belching smoke, and the two plumes entwine, creating a giant black cloud of smoke that enshrouds the tops of both buildings. It's billowing out and up at high speed and the breeze is pushing it at a low angle off to the side, where it expands and turns a light gray.

TV cameras are at the site now, and there are fire trucks everywhere. Emergency medical workers are setting up gurneys and IV racks. People are pouring out of the buildings and walking and running away, while other people stand and look up, stunned.

Every time they show the buildings, I think, *Mike and Roselle are in there.*

My heart beats hard, and I feel fear. I

begin to pray. *Please watch over Mike and the others in those towers. Lord, keep them safe and help them to make it out. Get Mike home safely.*

I hear a noise by the side of my bed. A pair of soft brown eyes framed by two floppy, golden ears pops up over the edge of the bed. It's Linnie, Mike's retired guide dog. She can tell I'm upset. I don't trust my voice to talk, but I stroke her head. Then I remember. *Mike is not alone. He has Roselle.*

I feel a tiny bit better. Then the phone rings. *Maybe it's him!* It's only been twenty minutes or so. I know he is probably not out yet. Seventy-eight floors wouldn't go that quickly, unless he took the express elevators. Mike is safety conscious, and because of the fire, I think he'll keep to the stairs. Maybe he is in the stairwell, calling me from his cell phone.

"Hello?" My hand clutches the receiver, hoping against hope to hear Mike again. It's a friend named Mairead. She was already at work this morning but was sent home, along with most workers in the Tri-State area. She wants to know whether Mike was working in the city today. I tell her, "Yes, he's there."

Then the phone rings again. And again. As the word spreads about what is taking place in New York, people across the country, and I suppose the world, are turning on their TVs and watching the World Trade Center burn, and now friends and family are beginning to call. They all want to know if Mike is okay. And I can't give them an answer.

Time is passing quickly, and I am concerned that I get to talk to my parents in Southern California before they receive a call from one of their friends. I punch in their number. My mom answers the phone in a sleepy voice, and I gently tell her she and Dad need to wake up because something big is going on. Then I tell her about the airplane attacks. "Turn on the TV, and I promise I will call as soon as I know something about Mike."

The reporters are busy now, with events speeding up. President Bush, on a trip to Sarasota, Florida, makes a statement and says the country has suffered an "apparent terrorist attack." All U.S. flights are grounded. A plane crashes into the Pentagon. And the White House evacuates.

I get up, get dressed, and take Linnie outside, but I feel like I don't even have time to breathe. I stay in the kitchen and answer calls, always with the same unsatisfactory answer. And the phone won't stop ringing. Our closest friend in New Jersey is my pal from high school and church youth group, Tom Painter. He calls to say he's throwing his clothes in a duffel bag and heading over to my house. *Thank God.* I love Tom. He is one of those people you can call at three in the morning. For anything. *Help is on the way.*

The TV is on, and I'm fielding phone calls. I don't even dare go to the bathroom because I don't want to miss Mike's call. *I wonder if the fire is in the stairwell?*

There is chaos around the towers, the streets and sidewalks brimming with a mass of people running and walking in every direction. People's faces are pale and strained. There are airplane parts on the ground and papers everywhere, blown out of the buildings by the explosions.

The column of smoke seems even bigger and blacker than before, when, without warning, it turns gray and starts to expand out the sides. It almost looks like a nuclear explosion. The cloud grows and grows and metal pieces are shooting out of the building, and the whole thing falls, the top floors collapsing downward. In just ten seconds, one of the towers is down inside a huge, gray cloud. I freeze, my eyes fixed to the screen. *What happened?*

The TV newspeople are in shock, too,

struggling to describe what they are seeing. Finally someone announces that the South Tower has collapsed.

I keep praying and answering the phone. Although I know Mike's office is in the North Tower, seeing the other tower disintegrate makes me more worried. When Mike was without a guide dog for six months, people downtown weren't always too helpful. *What will they do when everyone is in a panic, running?*

Roselle and I walk as if in a dream through the streets of Manhattan. I want to put as much distance as I can between us and the crumbling World Trade Center. I want to talk to my wife. I want to go home.

Although Tower 2 has collapsed, our tower has not. Tower 1 is on fire but upright and holding steady. *I wonder if our offices are okay. When will I get to work in suite 7827 again?*

As I walk, I continue to brush off my clothes and hair, although I know I can't get all of the dust off. David tells me I have some blood on my face from some flying chips of concrete that struck my ear. I have the sudden realization that I am covered in parts of the World Trade Center, pulverized to a fine, silky dust. Not only am I wearing it; I am walking through it, too. I can't quite get my mind around that.

We've been walking about ten minutes when it happens again. I hear that same freight train waterfall sound. The vibration is deep, thundering through the earth and climbing up through my shoes and into my legs. I pull back gently on Roselle's harness, and we stop. Roselle is calm and quiet, pressing against my leg.

The rumble becomes a roar, though not quite as loud as before. I don't feel the same terror this time because we have put some distance between us and the towers. But my heart breaks. Our tower is falling to the ground.

For a few moments we listen to the sounds. Glass shattering, steel snapping, concrete crushing. *It's the sound of a building dying.* I don't feel the same adrenaline rush as before. I think I'm too tired. Mostly, I just feel sorrow. *What's happening to the firefighters who passed by? And the people above the crash zone? Are there people still in the stairwell, gripping that same rail and counting the stairs? What about the emergency workers in the lobby, standing in place and directing people out?*

A picture of my office flashes into my mind. Not a visual, photographic-type picture, but a three-dimensional image of the office, with furniture, fixtures, and office equipment occupying a precise layout. I know the location of every pencil and piece of paper, every wall plug and light switch, and every piece of technology in the office. I think of my framed picture of Karen (for my visitors to enjoy) and of Roselle's safe haven under my desk. My fingers twitch a bit as I think about my Braille writer from high school, the first piece of technology that let me communicate on paper. Throughout the years, it accompanied me to each new office, taking prime real estate on my desk. *Is it still in one piece?* Right now it's easier to think about a dusty piece of communications equipment like my Braille writer than the flesh-and-blood people still caught up in this catastrophe.

The noise begins to quiet, and another dust cloud crawls by. Thank God, this time the cloud misses us.

"Mike," says David, "there is no World Trade Center anymore."

We stand there, the three of us, not knowing what else to say or do. I am nearly undone. I am a survivor, but I feel no joy. I am numb.

Then I think of Karen. I haven't talked to her since that moment I called her in the office after the first explosion. She is waiting to hear from me.

I pull out my cell phone and punch 1, the number assigned to Karen. Somehow I get through. It rings once, twice; then she picks up.

More calls. People want to know if Mike is okay. "I don't know," I tell them. "I'm waiting to hear from him." I feel like I can't catch my breath.

Every minute, every second, I am praying for Mike and Roselle. I know my husband; he is resourceful and capable. He's great in emergencies, thinking through the problem and taking the time he needs to decide on the best course of action. But what is going on is so far beyond his control and something no one could ever really be prepared for. I think back to Roselle's reaction to the early morning thunderstorm. *How is she guiding? Is she afraid of the noise and the smoke?*

I'm still alone in the house except for Linnie and the cats. I can't tear myself away from the TV or the phone. Suddenly I remember the cleaning people are supposed to come today. *I wonder if I should cancel?* Usually I pick things up before they come so they can do some deep cleaning. The house is pretty messy right now. My mind begins to wander, thinking about what the rest of the day will bring. *If Mike makes it home okay, we're going to have people coming over. And if he dies, we're going to have even more people, so I better get ready for them.* I guess thinking about practical things like cleaning house for guests gives me a break for a brief moment. It helps me focus and gives me something to do so I don't think too much about what could be happening to Mike.

Then the other tower collapses, exactly like the first, into a giant, gray dust-and-debris cloud. And the phone rings again. "Hello?" I answer. My voice is hollow and small.

"Karen." My heart jumps. "It's me, Mike." Then he says the two best words I've ever heard. "I'm okay."

I give in to tears. There are days Mike drives me crazy, but there are other days I know we were meant for each other. I know what it's like to live with a limitation. My legs have been paralyzed since birth. Right before she gave birth to me, my mother became very ill with a kidney infection. I was released from the hospital before Mom was, and I think we almost lost her. Doctors weren't sure whether the damage to my spinal cord came from the kidney infection or if it was related to my breech birth. Neither Mike's parents nor my parents were of the litigation era, and although they might have had cause, back then you just didn't sue doctors or hospitals.

I was the oldest child, and my parents had another girl and a boy after me. My dad wanted to be a doctor, but the war interrupted his plans. He served as an army medic then came back and went into psychology and teaching. During the war, Mom and her sisters drove school buses. They not only drove the buses but also brought them home each night and serviced them themselves.

I did well in school and got placed in the gifted group. I went to college at UC Riverside and wanted to become a school librarian. I had been working at the high school library since ninth grade.

I also attended Council for Exceptional Children conventions with my father and got to spend time with gifted researchers. They challenged my goal of working as a school librarian, and I remember them saying over a glass of wine, "Do you want to work with people? Or things?" People, of course. When I researched graduate schools, there were three major schools of library science on the West Coast: UC Berkeley, USC, and the University of Hawaii. But all three were physically challenging for someone in a wheelchair.

I chose USC, but not for the School of Library Science. Instead I was honored with a doctoral scholarship in the School of Education, and I earned a master's degree in the area of mental retardation. I did my student teaching my senior year but again ran into very limited opportunities due to lack of accessibility for someone in a wheelchair. I graduated from USC and started my teaching career in a junior high school with students diagnosed with educational handicaps. Two years later, I got the chance to be a team leader in a new program at a brand-new elementary school in Irvine, California. At the time, the state of California was master-planning education and pushing the inclusion of all students with special needs in classrooms. All children were mainstreamed, and the services were brought to the children rather than children being pulled out of classrooms for special programs. Many teachers were resistant to the new philosophy, but I found it fun and challenging. My room had a mini kitchen, so many of the young teachers ended up in my room, where we shared soothing cups of tea and brainstormed ways to deal with particular kids with bizarre behaviors. After about five years, I moved to another new school and became a regular classroom teacher. I taught third and then fourth grade.

In 1980, I took a group of people to Oberammergau to the passion play and fell in love with the travel business. I eventually opened my own business focusing on accessibility and making it possible for people with significant physical disabilities to travel safely and comfortably.

Mike and I met in the early '80s at dinner with mutual friends. We were in our early thirties. Mike was working for Kurzweil and traveled constantly. I was working as a full-time travel agent by 1982, after taking a leave of absence from the classroom. I started handling Mike's travel arrangements. We went two months without seeing each other again because of our schedules, but Mike was relentless. He called me every single day.

We liked going to the movies together, and we really liked to talk. I had a comfortable feeling with him, like I didn't have to entertain him. He seemed to enjoy just being with me and talking to me. We just fit. After a few months, we just grew into a couple. One day he came over, and he was burning up with fever. He had just returned from a convention in Minneapolis, where he had contracted Legionnaires' disease. I moved him to my parents' house, and he lay on my parents' couch for two weeks. My dad took care of him because I had to work.

Mike never really proposed. One day we were driving near my apartment in Santa Ana, and the subject of marriage came up at a stoplight. By the time the light turned green, we had decided to get married. A few days later Mike showed up at the travel agency. I was busy on the phone with a customer, and Mike didn't care. He grabbed my hand and slid a diamond ring on my finger. "I think I have to stop talking to you now," I told my client.

We got married at Irvine United Methodist Church on November 27, 1982. Mike wore a white tuxedo. I wore a white gown with a high neck and a white hat. The church was decorated in autumn colors and peachy-pink roses. The wedding was scheduled for 4 p.m., and we were expecting about 225 people. But 4:00 came and went, and the church was only about half full. At exactly 4:12 p.m., the doors opened, and the church filled up as people rushed in. Hours later, we learned that the mysteriously missing guests had been out in their cars, listening to the USC–Notre Dame game. My dad also graduated from USC, so we were all loyal fans and excited that they won on our wedding day.

Dad pushed me down the aisle in my wheelchair, and Mike was waiting at the front with his guide dog Holland. We had two ministers because we couldn't pick between them, and we said traditional vows.

After we were pronounced husband and wife, Mike pushed me back down the aisle, out into the sunset. We all headed to beautiful San Juan Capistrano for a reception at our favorite Mexican restaurant. After dinner Mike and I danced to Anne Murray's "Could I Have This Dance (for the Rest of My Life)"? Mike kept saying over and over to anyone who would listen, "Isn't she beautiful?"

I don't think I've ever been loved by anybody as much as he loves me.

(And I hope he knows I love him back just as much. Or more!)

I'm not a man who cries easily. I can count on one hand the times I remember crying. But a sob rises in my throat when I hear Karen.

"Hello?" Her voice is quick and sharp. It's

higher pitched than usual. It's just about the best sound I've ever heard in my life.

"Karen, it's me. I'm okay. I am out. Roselle and I made it out of the tower."

I hear Karen weeping on the phone. It's 10:32 a.m., almost two hours since our phone call just after the explosion above my office. Then we are quiet, with nothing else to say just yet.

You know what they say about the two becoming one in marriage? It's true. Just like Roselle and I are close partners, relying on each other in a symbiotic relationship that transcends the average dog-owner relationship, so, too, do Karen and I rely on each other. We are both wounded. Our bodies don't work quite right. While I have been blind from birth, Karen has been paralyzed from birth. She can't walk and gets around in a wheelchair. She is my eyes, and I am her feet. We need each other. Like most other guys, I don't like to ask for help, and growing up blind intensified my natural bent toward independence. I've always been used to figuring things out, doing my homework and finding ways to adapt and even excel. But I need Karen. She is beautiful inside and out. She keeps me grounded with her common sense. She matches me wit for wit. Her creativity and wisdom light up my life. She loves dogs. And she drives me around. What more could a guy want?

Because we both have managed to thrive in a world where our needs are not often met, we are kindred spirits, two halves of one soul. And today, we were almost torn apart.

Before we hang up, Karen tells me what is really going on. There are terrorists — no one knows how many — carrying out a coordinated attack on the United States. There are four airplanes involved so far, maybe more. The first plane hit our building, Tower 1. Fifteen minutes later, a plane struck Tower 2, the twin to our building. A third plane attacked the Pentagon. A fourth plane is still unaccounted for. Every plane across the country has been grounded, and the president is in hiding. No one knows what is going on or what will happen next. New York is in chaos, the country at a standstill. And the world is watching.

I breathe it all in. It's hard to accept. We are quiet for a moment. Then I tell her I love her and close up my phone. I want to get out of here. David, Roselle, and I continue trudging north, joining the throngs trying to flee Manhattan by car, bicycle, and on foot. At some point we cut back over to Broadway and decide to rest on a bench at a small Chinatown plaza near Canal Street, called Chatham Square. We sit down near a statue of Lin Ze Xu, a national hero of China who battled the foreign-backed opium trade in the nineteenth century.

I pull out my portable radio from my book bag and start scanning AM stations. All of them are reporting on what is happening at the World Trade Center. The mayor is on, asking everyone to remain calm. He goes over the details, most of which Karen already told me. Then he fields questions from the press. We listen for ten minutes or so, Roselle asleep on my shoes. Then the mayor gives us direct orders. Everyone is asked to evacuate to points north of Canal Street. Our rest is over. Once again, we get up and head north.

David remembers a friend who lives in Manhattan, a woman named Nina Resnick. He calls and tells her what we've been through and asks if we can stop at her apartment. She agrees without hesitation and tells us she will meet us there in a couple of hours.

We walk some more, and at noon we find a small Vietnamese restaurant open. I order soup. The warmth is soothing, and my muscles begin to relax with Roselle asleep at my feet. David is too shaken to eat, but

216

the noodles are just about the best thing I've ever eaten. As I sit at the table, I feel almost like a windup toy that's been keyed up but is now slowly winding down. Suddenly I hear jets outside. Everyone freezes. *What's going on?*

Then from outside someone shouts, "It's the Air Force! There are jets on patrol." The entire restaurant bursts into applause. For the first time in hours, I feel safe.

12
A Brush and a Booda Bone

My only concern was to get home after a
hard day's work.

ROSA PARKS

We hitch a ride to Nina's apartment in
midtown with some people in a van. They
don't speak much English, but when they
see us, they know what we have been
through and are eager to help.

We hit the buzzer at Nina's building a few
times, but she doesn't answer. Grimy and
exhausted, we sit in the lobby and wait. Roselle slumps down between my feet and immediately begins to snore. I wish I could
join her. It's about one fifteen in the afternoon.

Thirty minutes later, Nina arrives, loaded
down with grocery bags. She had been out
shopping for food for us. The stores were
packed with people in a panic, buying up
everything they could find. Roselle perks up

218

and wags her tail, happy to meet someone new. We head up to the apartment and sit down. Nina turns on the radio for us then heads into the kitchen to unpack the groceries. For the next couple of hours, we eat, watch TV, listen to the news, and talk. Like the rest of the country, we try to make sense out of something that ultimately makes no sense.

After a while, David pulls his laptop out of his briefcase and begins to write down what we've experienced today. I left mine in my office in the World Trade Center. It is now part of what the reporters are calling "the rubble."

I want to go home but lower Manhattan is still being evacuated, and the mayor tells everyone else to stay put. Everything is shutting down, including the trains and buses. Many airports have been closed, and incoming overseas flights are being diverted into Canada. The borders have been closed.

President Bush announces that U.S. Armed Forces around the world are on "high-alert status" and that all appropriate security precautions have been taken: "Make no mistake, the United States will hunt down and punish those responsible for these cowardly acts."[1] The Pentagon announces that warships and aircraft carriers are moving into strategic positions around New York and Washington, D.C.

As I listen to the news, above all it's clear that thousands of people have lost their lives. On an average workday, 35,000 people are in the World Trade Center towers by 9 a.m. Estimates of the number of casualties fluctuate wildly, but later it will turn out that on September 11, each tower held between 5,000 and 7,000 people.[2] The lighter number is perhaps due to the early hour and the fact that the date coincided with Election Day as well as the first week of school. We won't find out for weeks, but eventually authorities will put the number of people who died in the attacks on the World Trade Center at 2,825 people.[3]

By the grace of God and my guide dog, I am not one of them.

A voice mail alert pops up on my cell phone. Karen has called, leaving a message that a friend of ours has made it home to New Jersey by train from Manhattan. After some debate with David and Nina, I decide to try to go home. David's plan is to head to a friend's place on the Upper East Side. If I can get to Penn Station somehow and if the trains are running, I can catch a train to New Jersey. If it's at all possible, I am confident that Roselle and I can do it. It will be nothing compared to what we have been through.

After thanking Nina for providing a safe haven, we start our journey home. David, Roselle, and I walk a few blocks and then make a happy discovery: the buses are running, and there is no cost. We hop on a bus to Thirty-third Street and Sixth then climb down and walk a block to Penn Station.

It's 5:30 in the evening when David and I say good-bye. Our parting is quick but emotional. We have been through hell together. Just a few hours before, we had started a routine day in the office. It has been anything but.

David has been a good friend today, and I hope I have been a good friend to him. I think back to the other people we encountered during the day, both in the tower and outside. As our paths intersected, I tried to help whoever I could.

The experiences of today, as nightmarish as they have been, are also an opportunity, a chance to learn and to grow. I'm not sure yet what the lessons are, but I know they will be there. As David and I part, I set my face toward home. Roselle and I need rest.

"Forward," I say to my dear Roselle. The station is packed, bustling with people fleeing Manhattan for safer places. We head downstairs and board a train for Newark. The train is packed. People notice the dust still clinging to the creases and folds of my clothes and Roselle's fur. They know we are fleeing the World Trade Center. They want to know everything.

Were you in the Towers?

Did you hear the plane hit?

How long did it take you to get out?

Talking is hard.

Roselle and I arrive in Newark, New Jersey, and switch to the Westfield train on track 5. I call Karen to let her know we're getting close. She had been standing by to drive the van and fetch us in Newark if the Westfield train hadn't been running.

At seven o'clock in the evening, we make it to Westfield. We climb down from the train, and my ears pick up the unmistakable sound of our van pulling up to the curb. Our dear friend Tom Painter is driving, with Karen seated in the back. The door slides open, and Roselle and I scramble in. Our reunion is joyous. I am home.

A few minutes later, we arrive at the house to an excited greeting from Linnie, my retired guide dog. She wags her tail, her whole body wiggling with joy. Then she sniffs us thoroughly.

I take care of Roselle first. I pull off her

harness and try to give her a good brushing to remove as much of the dust and debris as I can, but for once she won't stand still. She runs off like she's on a mission and comes back in a few minutes with her prized Booda Bone, a braided rope with a big knot on each end. Roselle prances around with the rope bone in her mouth and Linnie trailing behind, hoping for a game of tug-of-war.

I think over the day's events. From the initial explosion and tower leaning, to the stairwell descent, the mad flight from the collapsing tower, the trek through the dust cloud, the discovery of the subway station, the long walk through Manhattan, and the journey home, it has been a very long day. And while I am spent, Roselle seems to have recovered already. And she hasn't even been outside yet.

Later, in the shower, I relax as the hot water washes away the dust and the sweat. *I am alive. Roselle and I made it.*

Karen orders moo shu pork, General Tso's chicken, and egg rolls from our favorite Chinese takeout. When the food arrives, Karen, Tom, and I enjoy a quiet meal. The television murmurs in the background as the media rehashes the day, but our focus is on each other. There were several times during the day when I thought I would never see Karen again. But here we are, safe and together. And much of the credit goes to Roselle.

My body begins to tingle with fatigue, and I head upstairs to bed. Roselle takes her place on the floor next to my side of the bed. She sleeps peacefully. The storm is over.

After September 11, everything changed. Thousands perished. For some reason Roselle and I survived.

When I woke up the next morning, my emotions were numb, but my body was not. I could barely move. Every muscle ached, and I was so stiff it took me ten minutes to get out of bed. I released Roselle and Linnie from their tie-downs, and they began bouncing around the room, winding themselves up for a game of chase. I moaned and groaned as I pulled on my robe and tied the belt, then bit my tongue so I didn't wake up Karen.

Even my hands were sore. I shuffled across the room and down the hall, the dogs running ahead. Each step was agony. My calves, thighs, and hips screamed in protest. I thought back to the long, long stairwell. *No marching briskly down seventy-eight flights of stairs for me today. I would have a hard time making it down.*

I took Karen's elevator downstairs to let the dogs out then limped around the kitchen and put on some hot water for a cup of PG tips. I was spreading butter on a toasted English muffin when it hit me. *There's no more office to go back to.*

I stopped, holding the knife over the muffin, and memories of the day before began to rush back, replaying in my head. I again heard the noise of the towers falling, the frightened screams, and the breaking glass. I shook my head, trying to clear it out. *Enough.*

I tightened my grip on the knife and turned my attention back to the muffin. There would be time later to think through everything that had happened. For now, I just wanted to enjoy my breakfast. And I did. It was delicious. In fact, I think it was the best meal I ever had.

Karen and I spent the day resting, fielding calls from friends and family, and consulting my doctor and Roselle's vet. I started on a course of antibiotics to forestall any looming respiratory issues from having inhaled dust and fumes. There were already reports about toxins in the dust cloud, including asbestos. Roselle's vet advised no special treatment for her, just rest and routine.

I also gave Guide Dogs for the Blind a call to let them know Roselle and I were okay. I asked them how to take care of Roselle. Was there anything I needed to do to help her recover from working through such a catastrophic experience?

"Dogs live in the moment," they reminded me, explaining that Labrador retrievers are so adaptable that they generally bounce back from traumatic events quickly with no lingering ill effects. And as Roselle romped around with Linnie, I detected no soreness or fatigue. If only I could say the same.

The realization reassured me. If Roselle's mind and emotions recovered as quickly as her body, then she was in good shape. There didn't seem to be any fear or timidity in her. She didn't act shell-shocked at all. I don't think she was reliving the sights and sounds of yesterday. She was much more interested in where Linnie hid the Booda Bone.

E-mail Message from Guide Dogs for the Blind
From: Betsy Irving
Sent: Wednesday, September 12, 2001
    12:22 p.m.

To: All Guide Dogs for the Blind
    Employees (all sites)
Subject: World Trade Center

We, in the Puppy Raising Department
at Guide Dogs for the Blind, thought
you would want to know this story.
Thank you again for raising an outstand-
ing guide.

I received a call from graduate Michael
Hingson with Roselle, Yellow Lab, Class
#606. He was in the World Trade Center
yesterday in the Number One tower on
the 78th floor when the first plane hit.
Luckily, the plane hit the other side of
the building. He and Roselle walked
down 78 floors to get out of the building. He, along with his staff and many
others, met firefighters going up. Shortly
after they exited the building, the Number Two tower collapsed, so they were
moving quickly down the street to get
out of the way of the debris. He made it
home last night about 7 p.m. after staying with a friend in mid-Manhattan until
the trains were running again. He said
Roselle was a trooper through the whole
ordeal!

It was a quiet morning. When Karen came

downstairs, she mentioned that outside she could see the smoke rising from the site of the World Trade Center, twenty miles away.

We were glued to the TV for most of the day. Reporters covered the ongoing search for survivors in the rubble, along with the national effort to secure likely terrorist targets, such as airports, power plants, government buildings, and bridges. We watched footage of firefighters, police officers, and Port Authority employees in shock and grieving their losses. Thousands of New Yorkers were out posting pictures of their missing loved ones in the public areas of Manhattan in hopes that someone, somewhere, could help them find the lost.

In the afternoon, I got a call that surprised me. Joanne Ritter at Guide Dogs for the Blind wanted to put some feelers out to the media. She wanted to know if I was willing to be interviewed. I agreed, not thinking much of it. Then she asked, "If you could talk to the host of any television show, who would it be?" Without thinking, I mentioned Larry King.

The next day Joanne called back and said Larry's people would be calling. Friday night, Roselle and I were in the Green Room at CNN's New York studios with Karen and Tom Painter. I felt more than a little overwhelmed. Monday had been a normal workday. Tuesday had been hell. Wednesday and Thursday I was exhausted and in shock. And here it was Friday, and I was about to tell my story to Larry King and his millions of viewers around the world.

E-mail Message from Roselle's Puppy Raisers

From: Kay and Ted Stern
Sent: Friday, September 14, 2001
To: Michael Hingson
Subject: Thank God

We just heard from Guide Dogs for the Blind that you and Roselle are safe and that you both had a truly harrowing escape from your World Trade Center offices. We are so thankful and proud of you two partners to be able to work together and survive under the most testing of circumstances. We had sent you an email immediately after the attack and not hearing a response were very concerned. We are so relieved that you both are okay. Amidst the sadness we all have much for which to be grateful. We are sitting here embracing our nine-week-old service dog puppy that we are raising for Canine Companions for Independence and we all send you, your wife, and Roselle puppy kisses and hugs.

Fondly, Kay and Ted

If I had been thinking, I'm not sure I would have been so quick to respond to Joanne's question on Wednesday. But my experience with Larry King was a positive one. As always, he was warm and encouraging, engaging me in a conversational give-and-take that highlighted my blindness and Roselle's role in our escape from the tower. Afterward, I was glad I shared my story. Most of Tuesday's news was both grim and disheartening; if my experience could serve as a bright interlude in an otherwise dark and desperate day, I was grateful and willing to do it. Our country needed hope and healing. So did I.

New York shut down for a few days. While the rest of the world experienced the events surrounding September 11 through the confines of a television screen, the attacks and the catastrophic consequences had taken place in our backyard. Everyone knew people who had died in the towers. Their untimely deaths caused shock waves that stretched out far beyond Manhattan and the surrounding bedroom communities.

Then the funerals started. Some New Yorkers were attending four or five funerals a day.

The choice to move on wasn't even a remote possibility during the weeks after. Reminders were all around us. One poignant story came from a reporter who noted the large number of cars left sitting at suburban train stations around New York. Over the next few days, those cars stayed, abandoned and gathering dust. In many cases the owners would never return.

During the days and weeks after, my body recovered. I was able to sleep okay, and I resumed my daily routines. But it was not the same with my heart and my spirit. There was no more normal. First and foremost, I mourned the loss of life and the tragedy of the many rescuers who had bravely stayed in the towers, doing their jobs even as the buildings collapsed. I thought often of the firefighters who passed us on the stairwell, the man who delivered the ham-and-cheese croissants that morning, and the two women who had been so badly burned. I wondered about the people on the floors above us in Tower 1, the people I rode the elevator with every day but didn't know by name. Who among them lived? And who did not? I would probably never know.

I did get some good news, though. I was relieved to find out that all six Ingram Micro employees who had been in our offices that day made it out safely. And no Quantum employees were lost.

I was angry at the men who did this to us. Their twisted minds and motives are beyond my comprehension. I almost felt as though this group of nineteen people could not have been human; otherwise how could they have planned and carried out such an attack, resulting in deaths and grievous injuries to thousands of innocent people? I could not understand it. I still don't.

Friends and family often asked if I had survivor's remorse. I did not. I think it's because there is no real answer to why Roselle and I survived when so many others did not. Traveling down that path, even briefly, led to an endless chain of what-ifs. *What if the plane had hit the 78th floor of our building, like in the South Tower? What if David and I had remained longer in our offices, working to power down the computer servers? What if I had waited for help with evacuation? What if we had tried to get to David's car in the parking lot right across the street from Tower 2? What if the South Tower had collapsed in a different direction? What if a piece of glass or metal had hit one of us?*

My mind explored these questions and many others, but I soon gave it up. I don't have the answers. I'm not sure why I lived. But I do know this: since I am alive, I must be here for a reason. I agree with Billy Graham, who spoke during the national prayer service at Washington National Cathedral on the Friday after the attacks. He said that we may never know why 9/11 happened, but we don't have to, because God is the sovereign One. He uses each of us in different ways, and I choose to trust that he used me that day. I know he used Roselle. The two of us interacted with so many others; some I remember and some I've forgotten. I don't know exactly what will come out of the part we played in September 11. I may never know. But I do know it's all about planting seeds, seeds of forgiveness, healing, teamwork, and trust.

After the Larry King interview, I began to get other requests. One of the major weekly newsmagazines contacted me and wanted to do an interview at their offices. They asked me to show up in the clothes I was wearing on September 11. But the clothes had already been sent to the cleaners; in addition, the whole idea seemed tacky and sensationalized. I decided not to do the interview.

When invited, I did begin to tell the story and there seemed to be quite a bit of interest. Along with the television, radio, and print media requests came invitations to speak to groups in person. At first I was hesitant, and I wasn't sure what I had to offer. I walked down a bunch of stairs to get out of the tower. *So what?* Walking down the stairs shouldn't be viewed as incredible or heroic. But I began to see that there might be value in talking about some of the things I learned growing up blind that went a long way toward helping me survive that day. And people listened.

Within a few days, I started working back at my Quantum job again, first at home, then in rented offices in New Jersey. But my relationship with the company soured quickly. As sales manager, I was castigated for the drop in sales. Somehow the powers that be did not understand the working situation in New York. Many of my best clients were busy attending funerals, not purchasing computer backup systems. As a city and a region, we were struggling to get back on our feet and find a new normal. It was going to take a while. But the pressure was on to focus on getting sales, and there seemed to be a suspicion from corporate that we weren't out doing our job. Even so, I exceeded both the third quarter and fourth quarter sales goals. However, the message from corporate was that not enough was being sold in the Mid-Atlantic region for their satisfaction. My media interviews didn't help matters. It was an extremely difficult time for me and for Karen. Both of us had been through a traumatic experience that we were still struggling to make sense of, and we lived and worked in a community that was still living out the aftereffects of the worst terrorist attack ever on American soil. The pressure I felt was tremendous; I have always taken my work very seriously, and I have always been harder on myself than on anyone else. But this time it was different. My priorities had shifted, and with the continued requests for interviews and speeches, I was beginning to get a glimpse of what my larger purpose might be.

Not long after, I got an offer from Bob Phillips, CEO of Guide Dogs for the Blind, to serve as spokesperson out of the campus in San Rafael, California. It was the very same place I went at age fourteen to meet my first guide dog, Squire. It was also the same school that trained Roselle. We took time to make our decision. Going from urban New York City to the lush green and gold hills of the Marin Peninsula on the other side of the country would be a huge change of pace. Taking the offer would also mean giving up my six-figure regional sales manager's salary. But I had changed. We had changed. The money and the demands and pressures of my high-powered job didn't seem as important as before. So Karen and I decided to take the offer. It was time to move back to California.

I worked for Guide Dogs for the Blind for six and a half years and had a wonderful time. From my office on the campus in San Rafael (with my "Dog Is My Co-pilot" poster) to the amazing people I had the privilege to work with, including Roselle's trainer, Todd Jurek, my term at Guide Dogs was one of the highlights of my life. Being part of an organization that gives people back their confidence and their mobility through a partnership with a guide dog is a satisfying way to make a living.

The requests for interviews and speeches continued to grow, and eventually I resigned from Guide Dogs and went on the road full-time, speaking to thousands of people every year. I will never get tired of telling my story as long as it helps people. And I will never get tired of answering questions. (Here's one of my favorites from a grade schooler: "How do blind people have sex?" Answer:

"They same way sighted people do.")

Roselle went everywhere with me until she retired in 2007 at a public ceremony at Guide Dogs. They also retired her name; no future guide dog will ever be named Roselle. Over the years she's been showered with awards for her role in 9/11: the Heroes of Hartz award from Hartz Mountain Corporation, including a donation of twenty thousand dollars to Guide Dogs for the Blind; a British award called the PDSA Dickin medal, recognized worldwide as "the animals' Victoria Cross" and given to animals that display conspicuous gallantry and devotion to duty; the American Kennel Club's (AKC) ACE Award for Canine Excellence; and special recognition from Guide Dogs for the Blind upon retirement for "displaying exemplary courage, steadfastness, and partnership in learning." In addition, Roselle's name was read into the National Congressional Record in recognition for her service.

I've stayed close friends with Kay and Ted Stern, who were Roselle's puppy raisers. They took her home from Guide Dogs when she was just four months old and kept her for ten months of basic training. As you can imagine, they are very proud. "She is just a steady girl," said Ted Stern in an interview.

One of the questions I get asked often is how Roselle was able to ignore what was happening around us at the WTC to concentrate on guiding. While our close bond and our teamwork played a part, Roselle's trainer, Todd Jurek, said there is no way to prepare a dog to guide through a life-and-death situation like Roselle encountered on September 11. While Roselle's abilities are in part due to a combination of good breeding and good training, "she is a very special dog," said Jurek. "Most dogs in that situation would have flipped out, and that's the truth. She is just a pretty amazing dog to be able to guide you calmly down the stairs with all that commotion happening. People ask me, 'How did you train that dog to do that?' I just put her through the training, and the rest was her will and her strong temperament. Roselle was fun, outgoing, and loved to play, but ultimately she was always a good worker and serious in her work."

When she was still guiding for me, Roselle developed a serious health issue called *immune-mediated thrombocytopenia* (IMT), a blood disorder characterized by the destruction of blood platelets due to the presence of antiplatelet autoantibodies. The condition is an immune system disorder, most likely related to her exposure to the environmental toxins and irritants she inhaled in the midst of that tremendous dust cloud from the collapsing towers. We kept her on medication while she was still guiding to control the condition, but when her blood tests began to indicate changing kidney values, we decided to retire her. It was a very hard decision, but we had known the time was coming. Guiding is stressful both physiologically and psychologically, and we wanted Roselle to live a long and healthy life. After she retired, her kidney values went back into the normal range, and we continue to keep her on steroids, to stimulate blood platelet growth, and cyclosporin, an immune system suppressant.

These days Roselle is a senior citizen. The IMT has gone into remission. She's still joyful and loving, with a gleam in her eye, but her joints are beginning to get stiff with age, and she spends most of her time napping in the sun streaming through the sliding glass door at the back of our house. She always jumps up to greet visitors with her wagging tail and body and a kiss. And if I were you, I wouldn't leave any socks lying around where she can get to them.

13
SHAKE OFF THE DUST

Interdependence is and ought to be as
much the ideal of man as self-sufficiency.

MAHATMA GANDHI

Many of the key moments of my life have
revolved around airplanes.

The most obvious example is the hijacked
767 that destroyed my building ten years
ago. But there have been others, and these
airplane encounters always seem to propel
me in a brand-new direction.

I grew up beneath the wings of jets roar-
ing in and out of Edwards Air Force Base,
where my father worked. The base sprawled
out across Rosamond Lakebed, a former
bombing and gunnery range chosen for its
big, flat surface and the cloudless weather
perfect for flying. During the early 1940s,
the military began flight-testing the country's first jet fighter aircraft, the Bell XP-
59A Airacomet. Later, the rocket-powered

Bell X-1 was the first in a series of experimental airplanes designed to test the boundaries of flight, and on October 14, 1947, fearless test pilot Chuck Yeager became the first man ever to break the sound barrier, in the X-1. This dustbowl in the high desert was the center of aviation research and advanced flying. Test pilot Scott Crossfield called this jet playground "an Indianapolis without rules."

By the time my family moved to Palmdale, about an hour's drive away, the test pilots were riding these rocket planes over 100,000 feet in the air and exceeding Mach 3, or about 2,000 miles per hour. Fighter jets such as the F-100 Super Sabre and the F-102 Delta Dagger streaked and boomed through the skies. At the very same time, I was riding through the streets of Palmdale on my bicycle, testing my own speed and sound boundaries under the shadow of their wings. I grew curious about the science of flight and how engineers used the laws of the universe to blast these pilots up into the edge of space.

I didn't get to ride in an airplane until I was fourteen, on my way back from Guide Dogs for the Blind with Squire. Somehow he wedged his big golden retriever body under the seat in front of me and spent the next hour cozy and asleep, his head on my feet. As the plane lifted off, I remember thinking, *Now I can do most anything I want to do.* I felt free and alive. Having a guide dog for the first time was like breaking the sound barrier, and I knew my life would never be the same.

After college, I flew all over the country for business, and airplanes became as familiar as trains or taxicabs. I loved flying, until a plane tried to kill me. I was booked on American Airlines Flight 191 from Chicago to Los Angeles on May 25, 1979. But I finished my work a day early and exchanged my ticket for an earlier flight. The next day I was in a Los Angeles cab when I heard the report. Flight 191 had crashed shortly after takeoff, killing all 271 people on board, plus two on the ground. The left engine had fallen off the plane, and the aircraft had rolled over before crashing in a huge fireball in an open field less than a mile from Chicago O'Hare International Airport. The accident is now considered one of the ten worst airplane crashes in history. I should have been aboard.

After that, I began to look at life a little differently. My family became more precious. I took my faith more seriously and pondered my purpose in life.

A little over a year later, I was thrown off of an airplane. In the early '80s, some airlines had begun harassing blind passengers, segregating them in bulkhead seats, taking away their white canes and stowing them in overhead bins, and forcing them to demonstrate their capacity to buckle and unbuckle seat belts. Blind people felt uncomfortable and in some cases were ejected from planes for refusing bulkhead seats.

In September 1980, I was refused boarding on a plane to San Francisco because the bulkhead seats were already taken. I waited for the next flight out and tried to board. Again, I was ordered to sit in a bulkhead seat. I refused. After discussions with the flight attendants, the captain, and the supervisor of ground personnel, I was forcibly ejected from the plane. My left arm was bent behind my back, my thumb was injured, and my watch was broken off my wrist. It was humiliating.

Most of the time, I prefer to defuse uncomfortable situations with humor, engaging people and trying to help keep every interaction positive. For example, airport security personnel often don't know what to do with a guide dog and cause unnecessary delays by putting us through extra security checks. I have a choice to make. I can seethe with anger at the injustice, but if I went that route, I'd be angry most of the time. The truth is, I face discrimination every day. But persistent anger isn't productive, and it isn't fair to people who just don't know any better. So I choose engagement. When security puts us through the wringer, I make light of it: "Go ahead and frisk Roselle. She loves it. Frisk her more!"

But that day on the airplane, my approach didn't work. They were treating me like I was weak and helpless, and it was time to take a stand, just like my parents did when I got kicked off the school bus. Most people have no clue how blind people survive and function every day in the light-dependent world. When you are blind, most everything is risky. The world isn't set up with us in mind. But we can and do cope. We use work-arounds, technology, creativity, persistence, and intelligence to overcome the barriers put in our way.

Later, I discovered the airline that ejected me had no blind seating regulation and that a blind person with a guide dog was allowed to sit in any seat on the aircraft. I was asked to testify about my experience at a public symposium with representatives of the Federal Aviation Administration and Delta Airlines.

Twenty years later, I was at work in the World Trade Center when four planes were hijacked and used to attack our country on September 11, 2001. The country has never been the same. Neither have I. There is grief and loss. There is also an opportunity for change and a chance to move forward. But to do that, we need to work together. That's how the terrorists succeeded, with nineteen people functioning as a cohesive unit and demonstrating teamwork by planning, coordinating, and working together in secret to carry out the deadly attack.

To fight back, we must work together or suffer from our lack of unity and compassion for others, especially those who might look or act different from us. A wise man once said that all of us have disabilities; it's just that most of them are invisible.

I am often asked if I believe that blind and other disabled persons are better off today than in the past. In some ways, I believe that we are. For example, Braille is easier and cheaper to produce now. Technology offers new ways to access information, travel more independently than ever, and, in general, live life with less difficulty than before.

But on the other hand, are blind people more socially integrated into society than we were fifty, twenty, or even ten years ago? I think not. I will know that I am truly integrated into society when people are interested in me because of something I accomplish rather than some routine task that appears daunting just because I am blind. I will know that I'm a real first-class citizen when I can walk into restaurants with friends and the servers ask me for my order rather than asking my sighted colleagues, "What does he want?" I will know that I have arrived when I can go to meetings or conventions where all the materials given to sighted people are automatically available to me in Braille or another accessible form. True and full integration is not easy. It starts with desire, continues with education, and comes full circle grounded in trust.

On that fateful day ten years ago, I trusted Roselle. And Roselle trusted me. We survived through trust and teamwork.

Recently I flew to Amsterdam to speak at a guide dog school. The event planners splurged and booked me first class. When I boarded, I relaxed down into the comfortable, padded recliner. I leaned back and put up my feet. My new guide dog, Africa, was curled up under the seat in front. But when I reclined, she lifted her head. I knew what she wanted. I patted my knees. "Africa, come!" Quick as a flash she unfolded her long legs and emerged, then hopped up in my lap. All sixty-five pounds. I stroked her head. *So much wisdom.*

Guide Dog Wisdom

What I Learned from Roselle on 9/11

1. There's a time to work and a time to play. Know the difference. When the harness goes on, it's time to work. Work hard; others are depending on you.

2. Focus in and use all of your senses. Learn to tell the difference between a harmless thunderstorm and a true emergency. Don't let your sight get in the way of your vision.

3. Sometimes the way is hard, but if you work together, someone will pass along a water bottle just when you need it.

4. Always, but always, kiss firefighters.

5. Ignore distractions. There's more to life than playing fetch or chasing tennis balls.

6. Listen carefully to those who are wiser and more experienced than you. They'll help you find the way.

7. Don't stop until work is over. Sometimes being a hero is just doing your job.

8. The dust cloud won't last forever. Keep going and look for the way out. It will come.

9. Shake off the dust and move on. Remember the first guide dog command? "Forward."

10. When work is over, play hard with your

friends. And don't forget to share your Booda Bone.

14
IT'S ALL WORTH IT

God does not present insurmountable
problems. Instead, he gives us
challenges, waits for us to overcome
them, and then rejoices.
MICHAEL HINGSON

There were several moments on September
11 when I didn't know if I would survive.
When the building tipped and I thought we
were going to fall to the street, seventy-eight
stories below, I didn't think I was going to
make it. When Tower 2 collapsed, I thought
I was going to be crushed by flying debris
or by the tower itself. And when the dust
cloud swept over us, I felt sure I would
drown. But I did not. Somewhere deep
inside was a tiny fragment of faith that if
Roselle and I worked together, we would be
okay. And somehow we walked out of that
cloud and survived. There are days I still
can't believe I'm alive.

I walked away from Ground Zero a much different man from the one who unlocked the office door that morning. I survived, and I'm okay, but I've changed. I don't think there is one person who witnessed the events of 9/11 who wasn't changed. There are those who have lost hope, who have grown bitter, angry, intolerant, and hateful. I am not one of those people. I still believe in dreams. I still think that if we work together, things will turn out all right. I still feel that if we each treat each other with kindness, dignity, and respect, we will live happily ever after. I have hope.

Not long ago, I was in line to go through security at the airport in Oakland, California. As soon as I got in line, another passenger said, "We're going to lift the rope and let you go up to the front of the line."

"Why would I want to do that?" I said.

"Well, it's going to be easier for you."

"What could be easier than standing in line? I do it every week. Don't worry about it."

"Well, it's easier on your dog."

"No, it's okay. Don't worry about it."

As we inched forward, three other people tried to move me up to the front of the line. They were insistent, and before long they became so angry when I chose to stay in place that I was convinced we might come to fisticuffs.

I know they had the best of intentions. I know they were only trying to help. But I didn't need to go to the front of the line just because I am blind. I want to stand in line. I want to move forward like everyone else. I don't want to be set apart. I want to interact with people, talk to people, and be with people.

I look forward to the day that I can go to the airport, stand in line, and not receive grief.

I look forward to the day when I want to cut in line and someone says, "Well, who made *you* king?"

I look forward to the day when blind people will be treated as equals in society, when we are truly accepted as first-class citizens.

Since 9/11 I've been asked to talk about what happened to me that day, and I made the decision to speak about it for three reasons. First, if it would help people better understand blindness and the fact that the handicap is not being blind but rather the attitudes and misconceptions people have about blindness, then it would be worth it.

Second, if it would help people understand how the guide dog relationship works, it would be worth it.

And third, if it would help people move on from 9/11 and discover some of the important lessons to be learned, then it's worth it.

Several years ago, I flew to New Zealand to tell my story. My second week down there, I spoke to a group of students in South Island who were active in the Royal Foundation of the Blind. After I spoke, one of them shared this story. He and a group of blind friends had recently gone on an adventure expedition. At the end of their trip, they had been sitting around a campfire when their guide got up and said, "I have to tell you a story. Before we left, I was going to call your leaders and tell them the trip was off because I did not think there was any way I could guide a bunch of blind people without someone getting killed. There was no way blind people could do river rafting and rock climbing. But then I watched a television interview of this blind bloke who survived 9/11 and came over here to show us what blind people can do. It changed my mind. I've had the best day of my life. I'll guide you guys anytime."

If this was the only thing this "blind bloke" ever accomplished by telling my story, it would be worth it. It's all worth it.

ter that year I spoke at Temple Univer- and a woman came up to me. She had a friend who perished in the attack on the Pentagon, and she was devastated, stuck, unable to talk about the tragedy. "I have had a hard time dealing with the loss of my best friend," she said. "But listening to your story and hearing what you learned and how you survived has helped me. You are right. We need to continue to dream, and we need to learn how to work with each other, and I'm going to do it. I can talk about it now, and I'm going to move on."

We can't let fear paralyze us. We must carry on. The best way we can honor those we lost in the fires of September 11 is by moving forward and building a better society through trust and teamwork. We can make it happen.

We need to dream, to dare, and to do. I lived a nightmare at Ground Zero, but even a nightmare can turn into a happy ending if we refuse to give in to fear. Out of the ashes and rubble of 9/11, we can create building blocks for the future. Don't let your sight get in the way of your vision. Join Roselle, Karen, and me. Let's shake off the dust and move on.

rward.

ACKNOWLEDGMENTS

MICHAEL HINGSON: So many people, blind and sighted alike, went into making this book possible through their involvement with my life that it is hard to know where to begin to name them all. While many of them are mentioned throughout the book, some deserve special attention.

First Susy Flory, my author colleague, has spent countless hours in learning about the world of blindness in order to help me articulate my story and to give you a more accurate picture of what it really means to be blind, which is much different from the traditional stereotype held by most people.

I wish to thank my parents, who stuck to their guns and didn't allow society to dictate how they should raise a blind child. Without the philosophy they gave me, I never could have survived and thrived in this quirky world that doesn't understand that it is okay to be different. Thanks also, Dad, for the many hours of stimulating spiritual talk and for reading me the Baird Spalding books and other stuff.

I wish to acknowledge Richard Herbold-sheimer, whom I met in my sophomore year in high school. He showed me that teachers are people too. Herbo, you are as much an inspiration to me now as you were in 1969. Your discipline and strength have stayed with me.

I wish to thank the late Dr. Fred Reines, my college academic physics adviser. Dr. Reines, you helped me see and prove that blind people could succeed at the study of physics just as much as anyone else. I am glad you finally got the Nobel Prize for Physics; you deserved it.

Thanks to the three great presidents of the National Federation of the Blind, Dr. Jacobus tenBroek, Dr. Kenneth Jernigan, and Dr. Marc Maurer, for your inspiration and strength in leading the NFB and so many of us into a better place.

I wish to acknowledge Ginger Crowley for her efforts to help me become a better public speaker and storyteller.

I also wish to thank Joanne Ritter, director of marketing and communications at Guide Dogs for the Blind, and her cohort in crime, Morry Angel, for making all this possible by seeing the value of telling my story to the world after 9/11.

I wish to acknowledge the invaluable assistance of all those who gave of their time to be interviewed for this book. Your contributions are great!

Thanks to all who read and commented on the drafts of this endeavor. You have made this a better story, and you have taught me a lot.

Thanks to Chip MacGregor, my agent, who guided me through the muddles of the literary publishing world. You truly are a wizard, and I am with you — Mark Twain is the best American author, bar none.

Finally, thanks to Bryan Norman, Brian Hampton, and all the wonderful folks at Thomas Nelson Publishers for listening and for agreeing to take on this project. I look forward to working with you in the future. Let's do it again.

SUSY FLORY: It's been a wild and crazy year. In the spring of 2010, I was recovering from breast cancer treatment, including two surgeries, chemotherapy, and radiation. During those weeks of radiation, I began work on *Dog Tales,* a book of true and miraculous dog stories. One of the dogs I wrote about was Roselle. When I first sent

Mike an e-mail, he graciously agreed to a phone interview. After twenty minutes on the phone, I had chills. "Have you ever thought of writing a book?" I asked. He said yes but that he also wanted a collaborator. More chills. I found out we both love travel, books, and dogs. And we live less than an hour apart. We decided to work together, and I spent every Monday over the summer at his beautiful home on the Marin Peninsula, just across from San Francisco. I fell in love with his wonderful wife, Karen, and their three yellow Labs: Fantasia, Africa, and Roselle. The dogs mob me every time I walk in the front door, and I love it. Michael, thank you for the privilege of working with you on *Thunder Dog.* It's been a blast.

My love and thanks to Robert, Ethan, and Teddy. You are Team Flory, and I love you. Thanks for believing in me and listening to all my dog stories at the dinner table. Mom, Sara, Jerry, Alice, Tracy, Mark, Dave, Bea, Jeff, Sheila, Teresa, Margaret, my dear friends in Homebuilders, and my Facebook and CAN buddies, thanks for praying for me and cheering me on. A special thanks to the Thunder Dog readers group: Leo, Joyce, Nancy, Mary, Kristy, Jeannette, Lorena, Marci-Beth, Jinx, Amy, and Kristi. And Kathi Lipp, my speaker chick friend, I love sharing this crazy writing life with you. A special thanks to Ann Dykstra at One Rincon Hill for letting Robert and me climb down the stairwell to get a little taste of what Mike went through on 9/11.

I'm grateful to Michael's friends and family who granted interviews and made me feel welcome: Karen Hingson, David Frank, Dr. Marc Maurer, Dr. Fredric Schroeder, Terry Barrett, Todd Jurek, Bob Phillips, Aaron Klein, Billie Castillo, K. Cherie Jones, Dava Wayman, Dick Rubinstein, Ellery Hingson, Hollybeth Anderson, James Gashel, Kevin Washington, Mark Riccebono, Mat Kaplan, Mr. Herboldsheimer, Robin Keith, Tom Painter, and his dear aunt Shirley Stone.

Finally, deep thanks to my agent, Chip MacGregor. I appreciate your wisdom and your passion for books that change lives (although I'm still not convinced Mark Twain is the best American writer ever). To Brian Hampton and Bryan Norman, thanks for believing in this story and loving Roselle and Mike as much as I do.

TIMELINE FOR
SEPTEMBER 11, 2001

12:30 a.m. In Westfield, New Jersey, Roselle wakes Michael, shaking in fear due to an approaching thunderstorm.

5:00 a.m. Michael Hingson wakes to his alarm, gets up, dresses, eats breakfast, and prepares for work.

5:45 a.m. Terrorist leader Mohamed Atta and associate Abdulaziz al-Omari pass through security in Portland, Maine, preparing to board a flight to Boston.

6:00 a.m. Primary Day election polls open in New York. Mayor Rudolph Giuliani is out, due to term limits. Charlie, the owner of Happy Fox Taxi, picks up Roselle and Mike for a ten-minute ride to the New Jersey Transit station.

6:48 a.m. The 6:18 train finally arrives in station after several announced delays.

7:15 a.m. Michael and Roselle arrive in Newark and transfer to a PATH train for the World Trade Center.

7:43 a.m. Michael and Roselle arrive at the World Trade Center station and walk through the underground parking lot on the fourth sublevel to an elevator that takes them to the lobby of Tower 1, the north building. Michael's security card is scanned by security, and they proceed to the express elevator.

7:50 a.m. Michael unlocks the door to the Quantum, Inc. suite on the 78th floor of the North Tower. Minutes later, David Frank and six other people arrive for the sales training presentations. One of the guests goes back downstairs to greet others expected to arrive. Remaining in the office are Michael, Roselle, David Frank, and five other people.

8:35 a.m. The Federal Aviation Administration (FAA) sends a message to NORAD: American Flight 11 out of Boston has been hijacked.

8:46 a.m. American Airlines Flight 11 crashes into the North Tower of the World Trade Center (WTC 1), cutting through floors 93–99.

8:47 a.m. Michael calls his wife, Karen, to tell her there's been an explosion.

8:50 a.m. Michael, Roselle, and David enter Stairwell B.

8:55 a.m. The first burn victim passes Michael in the stairwell. Five minutes later, another burn victim passes by.

9:03 a.m. United Airlines Flight 175 crashes into the South Tower of the World Trade Center (WTC 2). Inside the stairwell, Michael and others hear nothing of the explosion.

9:08 a.m. Someone passes water bottles up the stairs.

9:10 a.m. A column of firefighters passes by Michael and the group, beginning at the 30th floor. Mike speaks to the first firefighter. The FAA closes New York City airports.

9:21 a.m. All bridges and tunnels in New York are closed by the Port Authority.

9:26 a.m. All nonmilitary flights are grounded in the United States, orders of the Federal Aviation Administration.

9:30 a.m. President Bush, speaking from Sarasota, Florida, says the United States has suffered an "apparent terrorist attack."

9:35 a.m. Michael, Roselle, and David reach the first floor and run through the fire sprinkler waterfall to come out in the lobby.

9:37 a.m. American Flight 77 crashes into the Pentagon in Arlington, Virginia, a suburb of Washington, D.C.

9:45 a.m. Michael and Roselle leave the

World Trade Center and step outside. The White House evacuates.

9:59 a.m. The South Tower, Tower 2, collapses.

10:01 a.m. Michael and Roselle find an entrance to the Fulton Street Subway Station and take refuge inside. A portion of the Pentagon collapses.

10:06 a.m. United Airlines Flight 93 crashes in Shanksville, Pennsylvania, 80 miles southeast of Pittsburgh.

10:17 a.m. Michael and Roselle leave the station, evacuated by a police officer, and go back up to street level.

10:24 a.m. The FAA reports all inbound transatlantic aircraft are being diverted to Canada.

10:29 a.m. The North Tower, Tower 1, collapses.

10:32 a.m. Michael gets through to Karen on his cell phone and tells her that he is alive and has made it out of the World Trade Center.

10:58 a.m. Michael, Roselle, and David rest on a bench at a small plaza near Broadway and Canal Street.

11:00 a.m. Michael listens to his radio and hears Mayor Giuliani telling everyone to remain calm. The mayor orders lower Manhattan evacuated to points north of

Canal Street, and he tells everyone else to stay home.

11:30 a.m. Michael, Roselle, and David stop at a small Vietnamese restaurant to rest. Michael has a bowl of soup. Military jets race by.

12:02 p.m. Michael's boss, Rich Dickson, sends an e-mail to his staff: "Michael just was able to get through to me by cell phone. He and David Frank are together and are being evacuated even further from the area. Both are a bit dirty and tired but OK. Both got out just before our tower collapsed. . . . We really thought we lost both Mike and David as we watched our tower crash to the ground."

12:45 p.m. Michael, Roselle, and David walk toward Nina Resnick's apartment. They catch a ride with some friendly strangers.

1:15 p.m. Nina is out shopping for groceries, so Michael, Roselle, and David wait in the lobby of her apartment building.

1:44 p.m. Five warships and two aircraft carriers leave Norfolk, Virginia, to protect the East Coast from further attack.

1:50 p.m. Nina arrives, loaded down with grocery bags. The trio and Roselle go upstairs and clean up, talk, listen to the news, eat, and write notes on the day's events.

2:49 p.m. Mayor Giuliani announces that subway and bus service will be partially restored.

4:00 p.m. Karen leaves a message on Michael's cell that a friend has made it home to New Jersey from Manhattan by train. Michael calls her back, then decides to try for home. CNN reports that U.S. officials have evidence that Saudi militant Osama bin Laden is involved in the attacks. (Osama bin Laden, who later claimed direct responsibility for the September 11, 2001 attacks on the World Trade Center, was shot and killed May 2, 2011 in Pakistan by U.S. Navy Seals in a covert operation.)

4:30 p.m. Michael, Roselle, and David thank Nina for her help and leave the apartment building. A few blocks away they board a bus to Sixth and Thirty-third, near Penn Station. All transportation is free. President Bush, who has been transported from Florida to Barksdale Air Force Base in Louisiana, to Offutt Air Force Base in Nebraska, boards Air Force One to return to Washington, D.C.

5:21 p.m. Building 7 of the World Trade Center complex collapses.

5:30 p.m. Michael and David say a quick, emotional good-bye. David heads to a

266

friend's place on the Upper East Side.

6:05 p.m. Michael boards a train to Newark, New Jersey. People on the train see the dust on Michael and question him about his experiences.

6:10 p.m. Mayor Giuliani asks New Yorkers to stay home on Wednesday.

6:37 p.m. Michael and Roselle arrive at the Newark station and transfer to a Westfield, New Jersey, train on track 5. Michael calls Karen to tell her he has boarded the Westfield train, because she is standing by to pick him up if the Westfield train had not been running. Karen and Tom leave to pick up Michael and Roselle. Outside, they can see the smoke from the World Trade Center, 20 miles away.

7:02 p.m. Michael and Roselle arrive at the Westfield station. As they leave the station, Karen pulls up in the family van with her friend Tom Painter at the wheel.

7:15 p.m. Michael, Karen, Tom, and Roselle arrive home. Mike unharnesses Roselle and tries to brush her coat, but she is more interested in playing with Linnie, Michael's retired guide dog. Michael showers while Karen orders Chinese takeout. Michael, Karen, and Tom enjoy a quiet meal and watch TV.

8:30 p.m. President George W. Bush makes

a television statement, saying, "Thousands of lives were suddenly ended by evil." He adds, "These acts shattered steel, but they cannot dent the steel of American resolve." Michael's friends and family begin to call. Michael is tired but talks to as many as he can.

10:49 p.m. Reports emerge that there were three to five hijackers on each plane, armed only with crude knives.

11:00 p.m. At Karen's urging, Michael debriefs through the day's events with K. Cherie Jones, a friend and pastor in Atascadero, California.

12:00 a.m. Michael and Roselle go to bed and sleep peacefully. No storms.*

* Timeline compiled from *The 9/11 Commission Report*, along with notes by Michael Hingson.

THE COURTESY RULES
FOR BLINDNESS

When you meet me don't be ill at ease. It will help both of us if you remember these simple points of courtesy:

1. I'm an ordinary person, just blind. You don't need to raise your voice or address me as if I were a child. Don't ask my spouse what I want — "Cream in the coffee?" — ask me.

2. I may use a long white cane or a guide dog to walk independently; or I may ask to take your arm. Let me decide, and please don't grab my arm; let me take yours. I'll keep a half-step behind to anticipate curbs and steps.

3. I want to know who's in the room with me. Speak when you enter. Introduce me to the others. Include children, and tell me if there's a cat or dog.

4. The door to a room or cabinet or to a

car left partially open is a hazard to me.

5. At dinner I will not have trouble with ordinary table skills.

6. Don't avoid words like "see." I use them, too. I'm always glad to see you.

7. I don't want pity. But don't talk about the "wonderful compensations" of blindness. My sense of smell, touch, or hearing did not improve when I became blind. I rely on them more and, therefore, may get more information through those senses than you do — that's all.

8. If I'm your houseguest, show me the bathroom, closet, dresser, window — the light switch too. I like to know whether the lights are on.

9. I'll discuss blindness with you if you're curious, but it's an old story to me. I have as many other interests as you do.

10. Don't think of me as just a blind person. I'm just a person who happens to be blind.

In all fifty states, the law requires drivers to yield the right of way when they see my extended white cane. Only the blind may carry white canes. You see more blind persons today walking alone, not because there are more of us, but because we have learned to make our own way.[*]

BLINDNESS: A LEFT-HANDED DISSERTATION

BY KENNETH JERNIGAN

You have asked me to comment on a seeming contradiction in the philosophy of the National Federation of the Blind. You tell me on the one hand that we say, "The blind person can compete on terms of equality with the ordinary sighted person if he gets proper training and opportunity." You call to my attention our statement that, "The average blind person can do the average job in the average place of business, and do it as well as his sighted neighbor." You remind me that we tell the World with great insistence that, "The blind person can lead as happy and lead as full a life as anyone else."

You tell me on the other hand that we say blindness need not be the great tragedy it has always been considered, but that it can be reduced to the level of a mere physical nuisance. You say that these two propositions seem contradictory, and that if you are to buy the one you don't see how you can buy the other. You tell me you are prepared to accept the fact that the blind can compete and therefore you're not prepared, unless I can provide valid reasons to the contrary, to concede that blindness is a nuisance at all. That is, any more so than any other characteristic of any other person in normal living.

Let me begin by saying that you have put me in a very unusual position. Ordinarily people want to argue the other way. Most of them say that it's ridiculous to say that blindness can be reduced to the level of a nuisance since it is obviously a major tragedy involving severe problems and extreme limitations not to mention emotional distress and psychological disturbance. You however deny that it is even a nuisance and ask me to come up to the line and prove that it is! Fair enough, I shall try. The very fact that you can raise such a question shows how much progress we have made. I doubt that anybody could have done it as recently as twenty years ago.

To begin with, even if we were to concede, and I don't concede it as I will shortly indicate, that there is absolutely nothing which can be done with sight which can't be done just as easily and just as well without it, blindness would still be a nuisance as the World is now constituted. Why? Because the World is planned and structured for the sighted. This does not mean that blindness need be a terrible tragedy, or that the blind are inferior, or that they cannot compete on terms of equality with the sighted. And we of the National Federation of the Blind, for instance, affirm that the ordinary blind person can compete on terms of equality with the ordinary sighted person, if he gets proper training and opportunity. We know that the average blind person can do the average job in the average place of business and do it as well as his sighted neighbor. In other words, the blind person can be as happy and lead as full a life as anybody else.

For an exact analogy, consider the situation of those who are left-handed. The world is planned and structured for the right-handed. Thus, left-handedness is a nuisance and is recognized as such, especially by the left-handed. Even so, the left-handed can compete on terms of equality with the right-handed since their handicap can be reduced to the level of a mere physical nuisance.

If you are not left-handed (I am not. I am a "normal"), you may not have thought of the problems. A left-handed person ordinarily wears his wristwatch on his right arm. Not to do so is awkward and causes problems. But the watch is made for the right-handed. Therefore, when it is worn on the right arm, the stem is toward the elbow, not the fingers. The watch is inconvenient to wind, a veritable nuisance.

Then there are butter knives. Many of them are so constructed that the left-handed must either spread the butter with the back of the knife, awkwardly use the right hand, or turn the wrist in a most uncomfortable way — nuisances all. But not of the sort to ruin one's psyche or cause nightmares, just annoying.

The garden variety can opener (the one you grip in your left hand and turn with your right, that is, if you are "normal") is made for "normals." If you hold it in your right hand and turn it with your left (as any respectable left-hander is tempted to do), you must either clumsily reach across it to get at the handle or turn it upside down so that the handle is conveniently located, in which case it won't work at all.

Likewise, steak knives are usually serrated to favor the right-handed. Scissors, eggbeaters, ice cream dippers, and other utensils are also made for the same group.

So are ordinary school-desk classroom

chairs. How many have you seen with the arms on the left side? Of course, a few enlightened schools and colleges (with proper, present-day concern for the well-being of minorities) have two or three left-handed chairs in each of their classrooms, but this is the exception rather than the rule. It succeeds only in earning the ill will of chauvinistic right-handers, who must use the desks when the room is full and the left-handed are absent. Of course, these occasional left-handed desks are the most blatant form of tokenism, the groveling gratitude of occasional left-handed Uncle Toms to the contrary notwithstanding.

In at least one case, it would seem, the problem of the left-handed is not just a side effect of the fact that the world is constructed for the right-handed but a real, inherent weakness. When the left-handed person writes with ink (the ballpoint pen was a blessing, indeed), his hand tends to smear the ink as it drags over what he has written. Of course, he can hold his hand up as he writes, but this is an inferior technique, not to mention being tiresome. Upon closer examination even this apparently inherent weakness is not really inherent at all but simply another problem created by society in its catering to the right-handed.

There is no real reason why it is better to begin reading or writing at the left side of the page and move to the right, except that it is more efficient and comfortable for the majority, the right-handed. In fact, it would be just as easy to read or write from the right to the left (more so for the left-handed), and thus the shoe would be on the other foot, or, more precisely, the pen would be in the other hand.

The left-handed have always been considered inferior by the right-handed. Formerly (in primitive times — twenty or thirty years ago) parents tried to make their left-handed children behave normally that is, use their right hands. Thereby, they often created trauma and psychiatric problems causing complexes, psychoses, and emotional disturbances. Today (in the age of enlightenment) while parents do not exactly say, "left is beautiful," they recognize the rights of minorities and leave their left-handed progeny to do their own thing.

(Parenthetically, I might say here that those who work with the blind are not always so progressive. Parents and especially educators still try to make the blind child with a little sight read large type, even when Braille would serve him better and be more efficient. They put great stress on reading in the "normal" manner and not being "conspicuous." They make him ashamed of his blindness and often cause permanent damage.)

But back to the left-handed. Regardless of the enlightenment of parents and teachers, the ancient myth of the inferiority of the left-handed still lingers to bedevil the lives of that unfortunate minority. To say that someone has given you a "left-handed compliment" is not a compliment to the left-handed. It is usually the left hand that doesn't know what the right hand is doing, rarely the other way around; and it is the right hand that is raised, or placed on the Bible, to take an oath. Salutes and the Pledge of Allegiance are given with the right hand. Divine Scripture tells us that the good and the evil shall be divided and that, at the day of final judgment, the sheep shall be on the right hand and the goats on the left, from whence they shall be cast into hell and outer darkness forever and ever. The guest of honor sits on the right hand of the host, and in an argument one always wants to be right. No one ever wants to be left behind.

Whether these uses of the words "left" and "right" are subtleties of language reinforcing the stereotype and bespeaking deeply ingrained, subconscious prejudice, or whether they are accidental, as the "nor-mals" allege, who can say? It may simply be that the left-handed are supersensitive, wearing chips on their shoulders and look-ing for insult where none is intended.

It is hard to make this case, however, when one considers the word gauche. The 1971 edition of Webster's Third New Interna-tional Dictionary of the English Language, Unabridged, says: "gauche . . . left, on the left, French . . . lacking in social graces or ease, tact, and familiarity with polite usage; likely or inclined to commit social blunders especially from lack of experience or train-ing . . . lacking finish or exhibiting crudity (as of style, form, or technique) . . . being or designed for use with the left hand: LEFT-HANDED. Synonym, see AWK-WARD. gauchely, adverb: in a gauche man-ner: AWKWARDLY, CLUMSILY, CRUDELY."

Whatever else may be said, there is noth-ing subtle about all of that; nor is there anything subtle about the term "bar sinis-ter," which comes from the Latin *sinistral,* meaning left-handed. The 1971 edition of Webster's Third New International Dictio-nary of the English Language, Unabridged, says: "bar sinister . . . the fact or condition of being of illegitimate birth . . . an enduring stigma, stain, or reproach (as of improper conduct or irregular status)." Supersensitive? Quibbling? Not on your life. Lefthanders arise. You have nothing to lose but your chains. They probably don't fit you anyway, being made for the right-handed. Look for the new slogans any day: "Left is lovely," and "Get righty!"

As with other oppressed minorities, the subtleties of language and prejudice carry over into the job market. I know of a girl, for instance, who lives in Kansas and who sought employment in a factory in that state. She was interviewed and passed every test with flying colors. The prospective employer terminated the interview by telling her, "You are in every way qualified for the job, and I would hire you immediately, except for your handicap." In outrage and indignation she demanded to know what he meant. "Why," he said, "it's obvious! You are left-handed. The machines on our assembly line are made for the right-handed. You would slow down the entire operation." This is not fantasy but fact. The company makes greeting cards. The girl did not get the job.

If, in truth and in fact, the left-handed girl would have slowed the assembly line, it is hard to see how the action of the employer can be called discriminatory. He could not be expected to buy new machinery simply to give her a job, nor could he be expected to redesign the entire factory. The "normal" person is right-handed, and it is reasonable for the factory to be designed accordingly.

Or does all of this miss the whole point? Is this not exactly the way employers and the general public think and talk about the blind? How did the employer know that the girl would slow down the assembly line? How did he know she was less efficient? Perhaps she had alternative techniques. Perhaps, in fact, she could have done the job better than most of the other people he had on the line. He decided (based on what he doubtless called "obvious" and "common sense" reasons) that she couldn't do the work. Accordingly, she was never even given the opportunity to try. Beware the "obvious," and look very carefully at so-called "common sense."

Do you still say there is no discrimination against the left-handed? Probably you do unless you begin to think about it, unless you get the facts — and even then, some people will say you are quibbling, that you are exaggerating. How very like the case of the blind. How easy to make quick judgments and have all of the answers, especially when you are not confronted with the problem or compelled to look at reality.

From all of this, you can see that the life of the left-hander is not easy. Nevertheless, his infirmity can be reduced to the level of a mere nuisance. It need not mean helplessness or inferiority. It does not necessarily cripple him psychologically. With reasonable opportunity he can compete on terms of equality with his right-handed neighbor. The average left-hander can do the average job in the average place of business and do it as well as the average right-hander.

So far as I can tell, there is no inherent weakness in left-handedness at all. The problems arise from the fact that society is structured for the right-handed. But these problems (annoying though they be) do not keep the left-handed from leading normal lives or competing with others. They are at the nuisance level.

Therefore, even if blindness (like left-handedness) had no inherent problems, it would still be a nuisance since society is structured and planned for the sighted sometimes when it could be arranged more efficiently otherwise. For instance, most windows in modern buildings are not there for ventilation. They are scaled. They are there only so that the sighted may look out of them. The building loses heat in winter and coolness in summer, but the sighted (the majority) will have their windows.

I think, however, that blindness is not exactly like left-handedness. I think there are some things that are inherently easier to do with sight than without it. For instance, you can glance down the street and see who is coming. You can look across a crowded room and tell who is there.

But here, it seems to me, most people go astray. They assume that, because you cannot look across the room and see who is there or enjoy a sunset or look down the street and recognize a friend, you are confronted with a major tragedy — that you are psychologically crippled, sociologically inferior, and economically unable to compete. Regardless of the words they use, they feel (deep down at the gut level) that the blind are necessarily less fortunate than the sighted. They think that blindness means lack of ability. Such views are held not only by most of the sighted but by many of the blind as well. They are also held by many, if not most, of the professionals in the field of work with the blind. In the *Journal of Rehabilitation* for January-February 1966, an article appeared entitled: "Social Isolation of the Blind: An Understated Aspect of Disability and Dependency." This article was written by none other than Dr. D. C. MacFarland, Chief of the Office for the Blind, Social and Rehabilitative Service, Department of Health, Education, and Welfare. Dr. MacFarland says:

Let me repeat a statement which I violently oppose. There is a slowly evolving fiction which can be summed up in the generalization, "Blindness is a mere inconvenience." I do not agree with this, and I do not know what to call such exaggeration in reverse. I think it has done its share of harm, throwing some very well-intentioned people off the track about what blindness really amounts to in people's lives.

It seems to me that Dr. MacFarland is as far off the track as the person who would contend that blindness is not even important enough to be considered a nuisance. I think it would be pleasant to look at a sunset. I think it would be helpful to look across a room and see who is there, or glance down the street and recognize a friend. But I know that these things are peripheral to the major concerns of life. It is true that it is sometimes a nuisance to devise alternative techniques to get the same results I could have without effort if I were sighted, but it is just that (a nuisance), not a tragedy or a psychological crisis or an international incident.

It seems to me that many of the problems which are regarded as inherent in blindness are more like those of the left-handed — in other words, created as a natural side effect of the structuring of society for the sighted. It seems to me that the remaining problems (those that are truly indigenous to blindness) are usually vastly overrated and overdramatized.

Blindness can, indeed, be a tragedy and a veritable hell, but this is not because of the blindness or anything inherent in it. It is because of what people have thought about blindness and because of the deprivations and the denials which result. It is because of the destructive myths which have existed from the time of the caveman — myths, which have equated eyesight with ability, and light with intelligence and purity. It is because the blind, being part of the general culture, have tended to accept the public attitudes and thus have done much to make those attitudes reality.

As far as I am concerned, all that I have been saying is tied up with the why and wherefore of the National Federation of the Blind. If our principal problem is the physical fact of blindness, I think there is little purpose in organizing. However, the real problem is not the blindness but the mistaken attitudes about it. These attitudes can be changed, and we are changing them. The sighted can also change. They can be shown that we are in no way inferior to them and that the old ideas were wrong, that we are able to compete with the sighted, play with the sighted, work with the sighted, and live with the sighted on terms of complete equality. We the blind can also come to recognize these truths, and we can live by them.

For all these reasons I say to you that the blind are able to compete on terms of absolute equality with the sighted, but I go on to say that blindness (even when properly dealt with) is still a physical nuisance. We must avoid the sin and the fallacy of either extreme. Blindness need not be a tragic hell. It cannot be a total nullity, lacking all inconvenience. It can, as we of the National Federation of the Blind say at every opportunity, be reduced to the level of a mere annoyance. Right on! We the blind must neither cop out by selling ourselves short with self-pity and myths of tragic deprivation, nor lie to ourselves by denying the existence of a problem. We need your help; we seek your understanding; and we want your partnership in changing our status in society. There is no place in our movement for the philosophy of the self-effacing Uncle Tom, but there is also no place for unreasonable and unrealistic belligerence. We are not out to "get sighty." Will you work with us?

RESOURCES FOR BLINDNESS

NATIONAL FEDERATION OF THE BLIND
From the Web site: "The National Federation of the Blind is not an organization speaking for the blind — it is the blind speaking for themselves."

200 East Wells Street
Baltimore, Maryland 21230
410-659-9314
E-mail: nfb@nfb.org
Web: http://www.nfb.org

AMERICAN FOUNDATION FOR THE BLIND

Nonprofit organization enabling blind or visually impaired people to achieve equality and access.

2 Penn Plaza, Suite 1102
New York, NY 10121
800-232-5463

E-mail: afbinfo@afb.net
Web: http://www.afb.org

AMERICAN PRINTING HOUSE FOR THE BLIND

The world's largest provider of accessible educational and daily living products with over 150 years of service.

1839 Frankfort Avenue
Louisville, KY 40206
800-223-1839
E-mail: info@aph.org
Web: http://www.aph.org/

ASSOCIATION FOR EDUCATION AND REHABILITATION OF THE BLIND AND VISUALLY IMPAIRED

1703 N. Beauregard Street, Suite 440
Alexandria, VA 22311
877-492-2708
Web: http://www.aerbvi.org

BRAILLE INSTITUTE

Nonprofit organization whose mission is to eliminate barriers to a fulfilling life caused by blindness and severe sight loss.

741 North Vermont Avenue
Los Angeles, CA 90029
800-272-4553
E-mail: la@brailleinstitute.org
Web: http://www.brailleinstitute.org

BRAILLE MONITOR:
VOICE OF THE NATION'S BLIND

A monthly magazine of the National Federation of the Blind. Available in large print, Braille, audiocassette, or by e-mail. Back issues are available online through the online directory.

510-659-9314, ext. 2344
E-mail: nfb@nfb.org
Web: http://www.nfb.org/nfb/Braille_
  Monitor.asp

DAISY CONSORTIUM

International association promoting the DAISY (Digital Accessible Information System) standard for talking books.

Grubenstrasse 12
8045 Zurich, Switzerland
Web: http://www.daisy.org

GOOGLE'S ACCESSIBLE WEB SEARCH FOR THE VISUALLY IMPAIRED

Web: http://labs.google.com/accessible

GUIDE DOGS FOR THE BLIND

Nonprofit, charitable organization with a mission to provide guide dogs and training in their use to visually impaired people throughout the United States and Canada.

P.O. Box 151200
San Rafael, CA 94915
800-295-4050
E-mail: information@guidedogs.com
Web: http://www.guidedogs.com

K-NFB READER: READING TECHNOLOGY FROM KURZWEIL TECHNOLOGIES

Software packages that run on a multifunction cell phone to enable the user to read printed material by way of scanner and digitized voice technology.

415-827-4084
E-mail: info@michaelhingson.com
Web: http://knfbreader.michaelhingson
.com/

NATIONAL LIBRARY SERVICE FOR THE BLIND AND PHYSICALLY HANDICAPPED AT THE LIBRARY OF CONGRESS

Free program that loans recorded and Braille books and magazines, music scores in Braille and large print, and specially designed playback equipment to residents of the United States who are unable to read or use standard print materials because of visual or physical impairment.

Library of Congress
Washington, DC 20542
1-888-NLS-READ
E-mail: nls@loc.gov
Web: http://www.loc.gov/nls

RECORDING FOR THE BLIND AND DYSLEXIC

Works with leading publishers and technology innovators to bring accessible materials to individuals with visual and learning disabilities.

20 Roszel Road
Princeton, NJ 08540
800-221-4792
E-mail: custserv@rfbd.org
Web: http://www.rfbd.org/alt

NOTES

Chapter 1
1. Alex Lieber, "How Do Dogs Sense On-coming Storms?" PetPlace.com, http://www.petplace.com/dogs/how-do-dogs-sense-oncoming-storms/page1.aspx.

Chapter 2
1. Dennis Cauchon, "For Many on Sept. 11, Survival Was No Accident," *USA Today,* December 20, 2001, http://www.usatoday.com/news/sept11/2001/12/19/usatcov-wtcsurvival.htm.
2. James Glanz and Eric Lipton, "How the Towers Stood and Fell," *New York Times Magazine,* September 8, 2002.
3. Nancy Lee, Lonnie Schlein, and Mitchell Levitas, eds., with an introduction by Howell Raines, *A Nation Challenged: A Visual History of 9/11 and Its Aftermath* (New York: New York Times/Callaway, 2002), 24.

Chapter 3

1. Reporters, Writers, and Editors of *Der Spiegel* magazine, *Inside 9-11: What Really Happened,* edited by Stefan Aust and Cordt Schnibben (New York: St. Martin's Press, 2002).
2. Martha T. Moore and Dennis Cauchon, "Inches Decide Life, Death on the 78th Floor," *USA Today,* September 3, 2002, http://www.usatoday.com/news/sept11/2002-09-03-floor-usat_x.htm.
3. Ibid.

Chapter 4

1. Reporters, et al, *Inside 9-11:* 50.
2. Ibid.
3. William Roberts, "Plane Hits Building: Woman Survives 75-Story Fall," *Elevator World,* March 1, 1996, http://www.elevator-world.com/magazine/archive01/9603-002.htm.

Chapter 5

1. David Frank, "America, 9-11-01," Mount Wilson Observatory Association Web site, http://www.mwoa.org/David_Frank.html.
2. Mitchell Fink and Lois Mathias, *Never Forget: An Oral History of September 11, 2001* (New York: HarperCollins, 2002), 46.

3. Reporters, et al, *Inside 9-11,* 53.

4. Guide Dog Users of California, *California Penal Code,* Part 1: Crimes and Punishment, Title 9, chap. 12, sect. 365.5 (a), http://www.gducal.org/law_cal.html, accessed December 8, 2010.

Chapter 6

1. Quoted in Ernst Peter Fischer, *Beauty and the Beast: The Aesthetic Moment in Science,* trans. Elizabeth Oehlkers (New York: Plenum Trade, 1997), 12.

Chapter 7

1. Julio E. Correa, "The Dog's Sense of Smell," Alabama Cooperative Extension System, Alabama A&M University, UNP-0066, July 2005, http://www.aces.edu/pubs/docs/U/UNP-0066/.

2. Jim Dwyer and Michelle O'Donnell, "9/11 Firefighters Told of Isolation Amid Disaster," *New York Times,* September 9, 2005, http://query.nytimes.com/gst/full page.html?res=9904E1DC1331F93AA35 75AC0A9639C8B63&sec=&spon=&page wanted=print.

Chapter 8

1. James S. Nyman, "Unemployment Rates and Reasons: Dissing the Blind," *Braille*

Monitor, March 2009, http://www.nfb.org/
images/nfb/Publications/bm/bm09/
bm0903/bm090307.htm.

Chapter 9

1. Nancy Lee, Lonnie Schlein, and Mitchell Levitas, eds., *A Nation Challenged: A Visual History of 9/11 and Its Aftermath* (New York: Callaway, 2002), 116.

Chapter 10

1. Kenneth Jernigan, "A Definition of Blindness," special issue (*Low Vision and Blindness*), *Future Reflections* 24, no. 3 (2005), http://www.nfb.org/Images/nfb/Publications/fr/fr19/fr05si03.htm.
2. Rachel Aviv, "Listening to Braille," *New York Times,* January 3, 2010, available at http://www.nfb.org/images/nfb/Publications/bm/bm10/bm1002/bm100203.htm.
3. Gene Raffensperger, "Kenneth Jernigan: Power to the Blind," *Des Moines Sunday Register,* June 2, 1974, http://www.brailler man.com/jernigan.htm.
4. Tracy Smith, "A Blind Army Officer's Challenging Vision," *CBS Sunday Morning,* September 5, 2010, http://www.cbsnews.com/stories/2010/09/05/sunday/main6837189.shtml.

5. Catherine Mabe, "Blind Artist Wins New York City Photography Contest," *Disaboom* (a network community providing information and resources for people with disabilities), September 9, 2010, http://www.disaboom.com/blind-and-visual-impairment/blind-artist-wins-new-york-city-photography-contest-exposure.

6. Kenneth Jernigan, "Blindness — A Left-Handed Dissertation," http://www.nfb.org/Images/nfb/Publications/convent/blndnesl.htm.

Chapter 12

1. Editors of *LIFE* magazine, *One Nation: America Remembers September 11, 2001* (LIFE, 2006).

2. Nancy Lee, Lonnie Schlein, and Mitchell Levitas, eds., *A Nation Challenged: A Visual History of 9/11 and Its Aftermath* (New York: New York Times/Callaway, 2002).

3. Ibid., 234.

GLOSSARY OF TERMS
RELATED TO BLINDNESS

Adapted with permission from BraillePlus, an organization that provides alternate format documents to print-disabled individuals. For a complete version of the glossary, visit: http://www.brailleplus.net/visually_impaired _resources/Glossary/.

Accessibility: Most definitions of this term emphasize the ease of use. In the United States, several laws govern requirements for accessibility. Each of these laws, and even portions of them, is overseen by different federal agencies. Each agency is responsible for writing and publishing rules and guidelines that implement the particular law.

Accessible Format: A term that most frequently applies to visually impaired and blind users of print material. Its partner term is "Alternate Format." Standard print is usually published in either 10- or 12-point fonts. However, 10- or 12-point type is completely inaccessible to those individuals with limited or no vision. The Americans with Disabilities Act (ADA) sets 14 point (5 characters per inch) as the "minimum" font size. However, many other resources emphasize that this font size is only a minimum and a legally blind individual may only be able to read the largest fonts starting at 18 point (4 characters per inch). At some point (around 36 point), a print document will become nearly unusable because of the sheer volume of paper required to hold the very large print. Imagine a novel, letter or government report printed with just a very few large font words per page.

Accessible Web Design: Accessibility in web design is a measure of how easy it is to access, read, and understand the content of a web site. Accessibility is complicated by different browsers, different platforms, use of speech synthesis or indexing robots, graphics, movie clips, and sound files. Consideration must be given to many aspects of the site including fonts, color, spacing, background colors, use of tables, and animation.

ADA (Americans with Disabilities Act): The Americans with Disabilities Act (ADA) is a complex set of laws. The law assigns regulatory and investigative responsibilities to various agencies. Each responsible agency has published its regulations and complaint processes. Complaints and/or lawsuits can be filed on any discriminatory act within certain time frames.

Adaptive Technology, Assistive Technology: In the broadest sense, this term addresses the use of some sort of tool to deal with limitations presented by a disability — wheelchair, magnifier, talking computer.

Assistance Animal: A generic term referring to those animals specially trained to help people with disabilities with various activities. Such trained animals and their use are protected under the ADA. No such animal may be excluded from lodging, public accommodations or public agencies. The use of a guide dog by blind people is covered by this provision as well as the use of a Hearing Dog, Animal Companion, and Service Animals by those with other disabilities.

Audio Tactile: Cutting edge technology that combines the use of a tactile (raised line) graphic, a touch screen or drawing pad, and computer software. A file is loaded into the computer that has commentary associated with different areas of the touch screen. The tactile graphic has raised lines that represent or lead to those areas that have commentary in the file. Speech synthesis software voices the commentary when pressure is exerted on the various areas of the touch screen. This technology is still in development but has shown excellent prototype uses for a variety of disabilities.

Blindness: Partial or complete loss of sight with visual acuity of not greater than 20/200 in the better eye with correction or a field not subtending an angle greater than 20 degrees. Blindness may be caused by injury, by lesions of the brain or optic nerve, by disease of the cornea or retina, by pathological changes originating in systemic disorders and by cataract, glaucoma, or retinal detachment. Blindness can be caused by infectious diseases and by dietary deficiencies in underdeveloped countries where medical care is inadequate. Specific kinds of blindness include night blindness that may progress to total blindness, color blindness (an inability to distinguish colors), and snow blindness (a temporary condition caused by the reflection of sunlight on snow).

Braille: Braille is a code in the same way that we understand Morse Code, sign language, and short hand. It is not a different language. Braille consists of "braille cells." Each cell is two dots wide and three dots high. When the cell is filled, it looks like a rectangle standing on its narrow end. The Braille Code assigns specific meanings to virtually every mathematically possible combination of 1, 2, 3, 4, 5 and 6 dots located somewhere inside that cell, and combinations of up to 4 cells. For ease of reference, the dots are numbered top to bottom down the left side 1, 2, 3, and down the right 4, 5 and 6. Throughout the educational materials and rules, you will see reference to "dots 1, 3, 4" or "dots 2, 5, 6." Since there are only 64 mathematically possible combinations with one cell, many dot combinations have to serve many functions and have rules governing that function.

Braille, contracted: Braille consists of a standard alphabet and hundreds of abbreviations and contractions. Using such symbols creates contracted braille, saving approximately 20% of the space of non-contracted braille.

Braille display, refreshable: These machines use various approaches to raising and lowering plastic or metal pins through a grid to create braille characters. Some such systems are only for use with a desktop computer while others have the functions of a laptop computer also built in. Some units have but a few braille cells while others actually have enough braille cell space to replicate an entire print monitor.

Braille Embosser: A computer-driven machine pressing braille dots into paper and other thin materials.

Braille, Foreign Language: Most written languages also have a set of braille symbols representing that language. Each language and nation generates its own sets of rules concerning those characters and the formatting of the document itself. In most non-English languages, no short-form or contracted braille is used.

Braille, Grade One: Previous name for the type of braille that is spelled out letter by letter. Now called non-contracted braille.

Braille, Grade Two: Previous name for the type of braille that uses abbreviations and contractions to save space. Now called contracted braille.

Braille Literacy: This term has been

adopted by the blindness community in many countries as the central concept for advocating that children be taught good braille skills at an early age. Advocates equate braille literacy with literacy for sighted people and point to some critical statistics to bolster their position. In the United States, unemployment for blind and visually impaired people runs at approximately 73%. Conversely, only 26% of the blind people available for work have jobs. However, among those with good braille skills, 90% have jobs. The logic then runs that if children are taught braille literacy, their opportunities for gainful employment more than triple.

Braille, Paperless: There are machines that use various approaches to raising and lowering plastic or metal pins through a grid to create braille characters. Some systems are only for use with a computer while others have the functions of a laptop computer built in. The amount of braille characters displayed varies.

Braille Writer, Brailler: Braille writer has become a common usage term referring to the Perkins Braille Writer manufactured by Howe Press. These machines are the workhorses of manual braille preparation. In using them, the index, long and ring fingers of each hand are placed on the keys to the left and right of the long space bar in the center front. Dots 1, 2 and 3 are created by pressing the left-hand index, long or ring finger. Dots 4, 5, and 6 are created by pressing the right-hand index, long or ring finger. To create more than one dot, the machine allows you to press those keys simultaneously. Paper is loaded from the back and wound into the machine completely before beginning. As each line is completed, the paper is fed out the back of the machine.

Demographics, Visually Impaired: Demographics are the physical characteristics of a population such as age, sex, marital status, family size, education, geographic location, and occupation. The demographics for the visually impaired population are changing rapidly. On a world-wide basis, many eye diseases once causing much blindness are now growing less prevalent with the introduction of advanced medical care in developing nations. However, as that number shrinks, the number of individuals living long enough to experience eye diseases of the elderly such as macular degeneration is growing rapidly. For example, in the United States there are approximately 5 million people over age 65 with substantial vision loss according to the 2000 census. When the numbers are in for the 2010 census, this number is expected to double to 10 million.

Eye Disease: Conditions that impact the ability to see can be caused by injury, by lesions of the brain or optic nerve, by disease of the cornea or retina, by pathological changes originating in systemic disorders and by cataract, glaucoma, or retinal detachment. Blindness can be caused by infectious diseases and by dietary deficiencies in underdeveloped countries. More people than ever are facing the threat of blindness from age-related eye disease. Over one million Americans aged 40 and over are currently blind and an additional 2.4 million are visually impaired. These numbers are expected to double over the next 30 years as the Baby Boomer generation ages. The leading causes of vision impairment and blindness in the U.S. include: diabetic retinopathy, age-related macular degeneration (the most common cause of blindness and vision impairment in Americans over age 60), cataract (the leading cause of blindness in the world), and glaucoma.

Guide Dog, Seeing Eye Dog: This is a specially trained dog that helps people who are blind as they walk about. The dog wears a specially designed harness with a handle shaped like an upside down "U," allowing the user to grasp the harness comfortably while walking. These animals are highly trained and must always be considered to be a working tool not a pet to be casually admired or petted by other than the owner. Beginning shortly after weaning, these animals are carefully watched and reared to exhibit certain characteristics (obedience, calmness in strange surroundings, passivity when around other animals). Additionally, their health is monitored since only the healthiest animals will be used for the advanced training and offered to a blind person for years of service.

Handicap: A legal term used in the Rehabilitation Act of 1973 that is essentially synonymous with disability as described in the ADA.

Impaired Vision: The definition for most legal purposes in the United State is 20/200 vision with correction in the best eye, or field of vision less than 20 degrees. (See Legally Blind.)

Legally Blind: The definition for most legal purposes in the United State is 20/200 vision with correction in the best eye, or field of vision less than 20 degrees. From a practical point of view, the visually impaired community talks in terms of "a high partial," "a low partial," and "totally blind." Someone with 20/200 vision can see what the person with 20/20 vision can, only he has to be within roughly 20 feet of the object rather than 200 feet to see it. That person should also be able to use Large Print or magnification to read fairly comfortably. Eyestrain will become an issue, however, in many situations. A high partial may or may not use any sort of mobility aid such as a White Cane, guide dog, or sighted guide unless travel conditions are difficult. For example, at dusk or after dark, a white cane may be helpful to find the edge of steps, ramps or the like. Low Partial folks will have a tough time with most large print and are more likely to use a mobility aid. Depth perception and glare can become major problems in travel for them. Their choice for handling print material will be limited to either audio presentation or braille. Totally Blind means a virtual lack of any sort of functional vision. Some people with minimal light perception may refer to themselves as totally blind although they can tell when the light is on in a room and startle the sighted partner by turning off the light. Mobility aids are common and the use of either audio or braille is essential.

Louis Braille: Louis Braille was the inventor of braille. As a child, he became blind due to an accident. As he grew and matured, he desired a written form of communication that would serve him as well as print for his friends and family.

Notetaker: First introduced by Blazie Engineering in the mid-1980's, these easy-to-use personal organizers allow a person knowledgeable in Braille to create documents, read text, keep addresses and appointments, access a list of special utilities, and do so almost a decade before the sighted found similar convenience in the Palm Pilot and Pocket PC.

Ophthalmology: The branch of medicine concerned with eyes and diseases of the eye.

Optometry: The art or profession of examining the eye for defects and faults of refraction and prescribing correctional lenses or exercises.

Optical Character Recognition (OCR): The computerized process of identifying patterns of pixels in an electronic file as letters or other parts of language such as punctuation. Most advanced software performing this task can also maintain the format of the original page, if desired, through insertion of various codes in the "Save" or "Save As" process. OCR with any software package can make recognition errors. Powerful OCR programs will recognize potential errors and offer the operator the opportunity to edit the file on the fly.

Partially Sighted: The technical definition of "partially sighted" is that one's best corrected visual acuity is no better than 20/70 in either eye, but better than mere perception of light.

Perkins Brailler: This machine is commonly known as a braille writer. Early in the 20th century braille writers were produced by Howe Press. They were expensive, noisy, heavy and needed frequent repair, however. The director of the Perkins School for the Blind in Massachusetts in the 1930s, Dr. Gabriel Farrell, wanted its printing department to produce a better machine. He found the man to do the job, David Abraham, teaching in their woodworking department. Abraham also had had training and experience as a mechanic and designing and building machines that manufactured stair railings. When Dr. Farrell learned of Abraham's ability with machine design, he asked Abraham to design a new braille writer with the help of Dr. Edward Waterhouse, a math teacher. The three men developed the specifications for the new machine. The brailler prototype was completed in November 1939. After World War II, production of the braillers began. That machine has changed little over the years and is the same brailler known worldwide today.

Retina: The light-sensitive membrane covering the back wall of the eyeball; it is continuous with the optic nerve.

Scanner: In simple terms, these electronic machines examine a piece of paper bit by tiny bit and determine whether that bit contains a color or white space. In a matter of seconds, the machine feeds a composite digital picture of the page to the host computer that can be displayed and manipulated in helpful ways. In the large print production process, using the raw picture file may be possible. The picture file can be enlarged and manipulated to create a picture file that resembles a larger font. However, many times such manipulation leads to spacing and layout problems that are irresolvable until the text is exported through OCR Software. At that point, it can be imported into one of many word processors or desktop publisher programs to create the desired end result. In braille production, translation software is unable to use the original file; so all files must be exported through an OCR package.

Screen Enlargement: Computer software controlled by the user to enlarge and increase contrast of letters on the computer screen.

Slate and Stylus: When Louis Braille began to create braille, he used an awl to punch bumps down into paper or other products. Over time, the awl's shape was modified into a stylus tipped with metal and usually equipped with a pear-shaped handle for ease of grasping. The slate evolved as a way to bring consistency to the position and depth of dots. Today's slates come in varying sizes — one short line of braille to one to cover an entire 6 by 4 note card. Two strips of metal are hinged at one side. The uppermost strip has rows of rectangular shapes stamped into it. Tiny scallops form the edges of these rectangles. The lower strip is covered with six dot rectangles pressed into the metal and pointing toward the table. The user places a sheet of paper over the lower strip and closes the upper strip and presses it into place. Small hooks catch the paper and keep it from skidding during brailling. Since braille is read from left to right and must be used with the dots raised, the process of using a slate and stylus requires that the user punch the braille dots into the paper from right to left, pressing the tip of the stylus down through the rectangular openings. The scallops along the edges of the stylus help the user align the tip with the dot beneath.

Speech Synthesis: This is a term referring to use of a computer software package, a sound card and speakers to create speech as a substitute for a computer monitor for blind people. In simplest terms, the software analyzes the data in the video buffer of the computer and turns what it sees into phonic components. Typically, the software has a dictionary of many words with their preferred pronunciation against which to compare the data. The user can control the portion of the screen to be reviewed, the amount of punctuation to be read, among many other features. When commanded to do so, the software sends the data to the sound card and the data is voiced. In addition, there are some independent hardware devices that connect to a computer and accomplish the same tasks.

Tactile Graphics: This term refers to those graphical representations that have been specially prepared for use by touch. Historically, such graphics were prepared with a wide range of tools and supplies — sewing tracing wheel, awls, string, and puffy paint, among many others. More recently with the advent of computer technology and sophisticated embossers, many graphics are being built through use of software and produced with embossers or specially constructed paper that reacts to heat.

Talking Books: In general terms, this phrase refers to any recorded edition of a published document (magazine, textbook, and novel). More specifically, in the world of visual impairments, it refers to the commercially prepared editions of documents offered to the blind community through various organizations, libraries, charities and educational institutions.

Transcription Software: Computer software that converts print documents into braille. The user does not need to understand braille to use the software but relies on the formatting rules built into the software to produce braille.

User Friendly Design: The concept of user friendly or Universal Design, a term coined by the late Ronald Mace, is to make products, services and the built environment "aesthetic and usable to the greatest extent possible by everyone, regardless of their age, ability, or status in life." This concept is used to describe architecture, interior and product design, information provision and technology.

Vision Loss: This term usually refers to a progressive decrease in visual acuity. However, it can refer to the sudden onset of substantial acuity decrease or total blindness.

Visual Acuity: This means sharpness of vision or the visual ability to resolve fine detail (usually measured by a Snellen chart). Visual acuity is expressed as a fraction. The top number refers to the distance you stand from the chart. This is usually 20 feet. The bottom number indicates the distance at which a person with normal eyesight could read the same line you correctly read. For example, 20/20 is considered normal. 20/40 indicates that the line you correctly read letters at 20 feet that could be read by a person with normal vision at 40 feet. The test is performed when there are problems or changes in vision.

White Cane: The Long White Cane was invented in the United States in 1930 by George A. Bonham. Its distinctive white length with a red band around the bottom is internationally recognized as a sign that the person using it is blind.

FOR FURTHER READING

Fink, Mitchell, and Lois Mathias. *Never Forget: An Oral History of September 11, 2001*. New York: HarperCollins, 2002. Personal stories by the survivors of September 11.

Flory, Susy. *Dog Tales: Inspirational Stories of Humor, Adventure, and Devotion*. Eugene, OR: Harvest House, 2011. Features seventeen true dog stories, including Roselle's.

Jackson, Donna M. *Hero Dogs: Courageous Canines in Action*. New York: Little, Brown Young Readers, 2003. A journalist looks at extraordinary dogs and the role they play in the daily lives of humans. Features Roselle's story.

Kurzweil, Ray. *The Singularity Is Near: When Humans Transcend Biology*. New York: Viking, 2005.

Lee, Nancy, Lonnie Schlein, and Mitchel

Levitas, eds. *A Nation Challenged: A Visual History of 9/11 and Its Aftermath.* New York: Callaway, 2002. A detailed visual, graphic, and written account of the WTC attacks in 2001.

Matson, Floyd. *Walking Alone and Marching Together: A History of the Organized Blind Movement in the United States, 1940–1990.* Baltimore: National Federation of the Blind, 1990. Includes an account of the incident where Michael Hingson was forcibly removed from a commercial airline flight for refusing a bulkhead seat, page 529.

Mueller, Pamela Bauer. *Hello, Goodbye, I Love You,* 2003 and *Aloha Crossing,* 2008. El Paso: Pinata Publishing. Michael Hingson wrote the foreword to *Hello, Goodbye, I Love You,* aimed at children in grades 3–7. Seventh grader Diego raises a puppy named Aloha to become a guide dog for the blind. Diego meets Miss Kimberly Louise, a woman who lost her sight in a car accident, when Aloha becomes her guide dog. *Aloha Crossing* is the award-winning sequel.

Murphy, Dean E. *September 11: An Oral History.* New York: Doubleday, 2002. Murphy is a reporter for the *New York Times.*

Features the story of Michael Hingson and David Frank, beginning on page 16.

Reporters, Writers, and Editors of *Der Spiegel Magazine. Inside 9/11: What Really Happened.* New York: St. Martin's Paperbacks, 2002. Michael Hingson and David Frank's account is featured beginning on page 97.

Sullivan, Robert, ed., and the editors of *LIFE* magazine. *One Nation: America Remembers September 11, 2001,* Fifth Anniversary exp. ed. New York: Time Inc. Home Entertainment, Time Life Books, 2006. Features a story on Michael and Roselle, page 132.

Sullivan, Tom. *Adventures in Darkness: Memoirs of an Eleven-Year-Old Blind Boy.* Nashville: Thomas Nelson, 2007. Blind since birth, Tom lived in a challenging world of isolation and special treatment. But he was driven to break out and live as sighted people do. Tom is now a successful actor, singer, author, and producer.

THE ROSELLE'S DREAM FOUNDATION

Equipping blind children and adults with the technology they need to live out their dreams.

Blind people today face a high-tech world. However, because the technology used to gain access to our world is often very expensive, blind people are sometimes excluded from the tools and technology that would enable them to live life to the fullest and to make their own contributions to society. That's why, in honor of my guide dog, Roselle, and the courage, poise, and teamwork she displayed on September 11, 2001, I founded The Roselle's Dream Foundation.

It's our goal at the Foundation to help today's blind children and adults not only to have access to the technology they need to excel in school and at work, but to live out their dreams. I have always wanted to do something to help more blind children get a proper education and have the tools to take with them into the future. I've also dreamed of helping blind adults get technology to do their jobs and live up to their potential. Through The Roselle's Dream Foundation, I want to make the dreams of blind children and adults a reality.

Michael Hingson, Founder

Roselle
9-11 Survivor & Hero

To learn how you can help put much-needed technology in the hands of blind children and adults, please contact:
The Roselle's Dream Foundation, Inc.
www.rosellesdream.org

ABOUT THE AUTHORS

Michael Hingson, national ambassador for the Braille Literacy Campaign, is a miraculous survivor of 9/11. He now owns The Michael Hingson Group, Inc., a consulting firm concerning inclusiveness and diversity and a platform for engaging speaking opportunities. A graduate of the University of California (Irvine) and a cum laude graduate with a master's degree in physics, Hingson has never let blindness stop him from achieving his goals. His life is a testimony to the power of trust, perseverance, and the amazing bond between human and animals. Michael and his wife, Karen, live in the San Francisco Bay Area with three yellow lab guide dogs, Roselle (retired), Africa, and Fantasia, and one cat, Sherlock.

Susy Flory is the author or coauthor of four books, including *So Long Status Quo,* a memoir about nine women who changed the world. Her articles have appeared in

Today's Christian Woman, Enrichment Journal, Guideposts books, Kyria.com, and with Focus on the Family. With degrees from UCLA in English and psychology and a background that includes journalism, education, and communications, Susy loves to uncover stories with happy endings that inspire and challenge readers to a life of passion, boldness, and adventure. She grew up on the back of a quarter horse in northern California and now lives in the San Francisco Bay Area with her husband, two children, and two dogs, Eli (a chocolate Lab) and Sprinkles, (a silky terrier).

The employees of Thorndike Press hope you have enjoyed this Large Print book. All our Thorndike, Wheeler, and Kennebec Large Print titles are designed for easy reading, and all our books are made to last. Other Thorndike Press Large Print books are available at your library, through selected bookstores, or directly from us.

For information about titles, please call:
(800) 223-1244

or visit our Web site at:
http://gale.cengage.com/thorndike

To share your comments, please write:
Publisher
Thorndike Press
10 Water St., Suite 310
Waterville, ME 04901